*Practical Experience*

Seriously useful guides

# Practical Experience

An Architecture Student's Guide
to Internship and the Year Out

*Igor Marjanović, Katerina Rüedi Ray, and
Jane Tankard*

AMSTERDAM • BOSTON • HEIDELBERG • LONDON • NEW YORK • OXFORD
PARIS • SAN DIEGO • SAN FRANCISCO • SINGAPORE • SYDNEY • TOKYO
ELSEVIER          Architectural Press is an imprint of Elsevier

Architectural
Press

Architectural Press
An imprint of Elsevier
Linacre House, Jordan Hill, Oxford OX2 8DP
30 Corporate Drive, Burlington, MA 01803

First published 2005

**British Library Cataloguing in Publication Data**
A catalogue record for this book is available from the British Library

**Library of Congress Cataloguing in Publication Data**
A catalogue record for this book is available from the Library of Congress

ISBN 0 7506 6206 9

For information on all Architectural Press publication visit our
web site at http://books.elsevier.com

Typeset by Charon Tec. Pvt. Ltd, Chennai, India
Printed and bound in Great Britain

# Contents

viii   *Contents*

# About the Authors

**Igor Marjanović** is director of the Core Design Programme and assistant professor of architecture at Iowa State University. Together with Katerina Rüedi Ray, he is principal of *ReadyMade Studio*, an interdisciplinary art and design practice, which is one of 10 selected exhibitors in the architectural exhibition *Ten Visions: Chicago Architecture* at the Art Institute of Chicago. Marjanović's work – as a teacher, a designer, and a writer – focuses on the appropriation of montage practices and critical theories in design. He has co-authored *The Portfolio* (Architectural Press, Oxford). His current research focuses on Alvin Boyarsky's influence on the twentieth century architectural education and practice. Marjanović graduated summa cum laude from the University of Belgrade, Serbia, and completed his diploma thesis at the Moscow Institute of Architecture. He also received a Master of Architecture degree from the University of Illinois at Chicago, where he was awarded the UIC/Skidmore, Owings, and Merrill Scholarship. Marjanović is a Ph.D. candidate at the Bartlett School of Architecture, University College London, UK.

**Katerina Rüedi Ray** is an Architects' Registration Board (ARB) registered architect and the director of the School of Art at Bowling Green State University, USA, and, with Igor Marjanović, principal of *ReadyMade Studio*. From 1996 to 2002 she was the director of the School of Architecture at the University of Illinois at Chicago. She studied architecture at the University of Dundee, the Architectural Association in London, and has a masters and a doctoral degree in architecture from University College London, UK. She has taught architectural design and theory at the Architectural Association, The Bartlett School and

Kingston University, UK, before taking up the position at UIC. Her work as an architect has won various European design awards and she has acted as a visiting professor, critic, and lecturer at numerous European and North American architecture and art schools. Her research focuses on design education, interdisciplinarity, and identity politics. Her co-authored publications include *Desiring Practices: Architecture, Gender and the Interdisciplinary*, *The Dissertation: An Architecture Student's Handbook* and *Chicago Architecture: Histories, Revisions, Alternatives*. She is currently working on several books, including *Bauhaus Dream-house: Identity Formation in Modernist Design Education*, and *133 and Rising: African American Women Architects*.

**Jane Tankard** is an ARB registered architect living and practising in the UK. She is a senior lecturer at the University of Westminster School of Architecture and the Built Environment, where she leads an undergraduate design studio. She is also a partner of *Tankard Bowkett*, an architectural practice specializing in domestic architecture and interior design. Her work, as both a practising architect and academic, has been documented in a variety of publications. She has worked in partnership with various local authorities in London advising on and initiating strategic urban design projects, and continues to be involved in urban environmental initiatives. Her interest in multi-disciplinary practice is central to her practice and research, which ranges from architecture to writing, furniture, and product design. Her investigations into cultural diversity, and architectural education and practice in the twenty-first century have led to collaborations with the Arts Council of England, the British Council and a number of Schools of Architecture in the UK and India. She currently lives in North London with her partner and three children.

# Acknowledgements

Throughout the enchanting labour that resulted in this book, we have been aided by the generosity, enthusiasm, and support of many colleagues and friends. To all of them we are deeply grateful. We want to thank Brian Carter of the School of Architecture and Planning, University at Buffalo, State University of New York; David Dunster, Roscoe Professor of Architecture, Liverpool University; Pamela Edwards and Chris Ellis of the Royal Institute of British Architects (RIBA); Frank Heitzman of Triton College, Illinois; Emma Matthews of Architect's Registration Board (ARB); Rob Rosenfeld of National Council of Architectural Registration Boards (NCARB), Illinois; and Kate Schwennsen of Iowa State University, who each read a part of the manuscript and offered outstanding advice, criticism, and encouragement.

This project would never have been possible without the generous contributions from design practitioners around the world. For their help and generosity we are indebted to:

- UK practitioners: Nicholas Boyarsky and Nicola Murphy of *Boyarsky Murphy Architects*; Alex de Rijke and Kate Burnett of *dRMM*; Andy Gollifer of *Gollifer Associates*; Andy Houlton of *Houlton Architects*; Gerard Cooke and Clyde Malby of *Davis Langdon Everest*; Jonathan Leah of *Alsop Architects*; Linda McCarney of *AHMM*; and Juliet Walshe of *Arup Associates*; a number of year-out students provided helpful additional text, including Panos Hadjichristofis of dRMM and James Hampton of Alsop Architects. We also wish to thank Stephen Brookhouse, Kate Heron, and Jasmin Sharif of the University of Westminster School of Architecture and the Built Environment for their help and advice.

- US practitioners: Calvin Lewis of *HLKB Architecture*; Douglas Garofalo of *Garofalo Architects*; Mark Robbins of Syracuse University; Daniel Wheeler of *Wheeler Kearns Architects*; Xavier Vendrell of *Xavier Vendrell Studio*; Trung Le of *OWP/P Architects Inc.*; and Louis Weller of *Weller Architects*. Lynn Paxson of Iowa State University provided us with knowledge and understanding of American Indian practices. Additional thanks are also due to Dr. Lubomir Popov at Bowling Green State University for his contributions regarding interior design practice.
- Other international practitioners: Ásdís Ágústsdóttir of *Yrki Architects*; Tomris Akin of *Mimarlar Tasarim – office of Han Tumertekin*; Gerardo Caballero of *Gerardo Caballero Architect*; Yongjie Cai, Zhenyu Li, and Zhijun Wang of *LineSpace*; Louisa Hutton and Karine Stigt of *Sauerbruch Hutton*; Anders Johansson of *Testbedstudio*; Roman Koucký of *Architektonická Kancelář Roman Koucký*; Mphethi Morojele of *mma architects*; Phil Mashabane of *Mashabane Rose Architects*; Alero Olympio of *Alero Olympio Architects*; Elsie Owusu of *Ghana Infrastructure Ltd.*; Ulrike Passe of *Passe Kälber Architekten*; Dan Shapiro of *Rolinet et Associés Architectes et Urbanistes*; and José María Torres Nadal and Edgar Gonzales of *José María Torres Nadal Arquitectos*. Particular additional thanks are also due to Ulrike Passe of *Passe Kälber Architekten* for her contributions on German architecture as well as her assistance in contacting a number of contributors. Our thanks are also due to Javier Sánchez Merina for his contributions on Spanish architecture and extensive help in reaching contributors. We also thank Lesley Naa Norle Lokko for her role in making contact with African practices and helping with texts on African nations. Other architects, architectural historians and critics helped with information and contacts: our thanks therefore go to, among others, Halldóra Arnardóttir, architectural historian, and Irena Fialová, architectural author and critic, for their assistance. Finally we wish to thank Mehmet Can Anbarlilar, Indraneel Dutta, Zane Karpova, Manuel Lopez, and Juan Manuel Rois, all former students of the University of Illinois at Chicago School of Architecture, for their extensive help in reaching practices in Asia, Eastern Europe, and South America. All of them taught us a great deal about the richness and diversity of practices throughout the world.

We are also very grateful to Catharine Steers and Alison Yates at Elsevier Science/The Architectural Press for their advice, criticism, and support, and Carissa Gavin and Nora Wendl, graduate assistants at Iowa State University for their insightful work on the cover image.

It is, however, important to add that with the exception of the texts describing architectural practice in the case study chapters, most of which were written by or in collaboration with the practices themselves, the opinions and interpretations expressed in this volume are ours alone.

The production of any book involves a network of support that reaches far into professional and personal life. We therefore owe a special debt to our colleagues, students, and administrators at Iowa State University, Bowling Green State University, and the University of Westminster. Finally, and most importantly, however, we want to thank our partners, Jasna Marjanović, Roger Ray, and Steve Bowkett, for their support and understanding. In many ways, visible and invisible, this book is a result of their labour too.

# List of Illustrations

# Introduction

## The Handbook

This handbook provides a guide to the process of finding, keeping, and making the most of the job or jobs you will need to complete your internship year or year out. It explains what to do, when to do it, and the major pitfalls you need to avoid along the way. It outlines existing requirements for the internship year in the USA and professional experience in the UK. It suggests ways in which you can, if you take time to understand the process, use your first few periods in professional employment to gain the kind of experience that is as close to your interests as possible. It outlines different kinds of practice that might fulfil your hopes as well as the expectations of professional systems in the USA and UK. We describe professional experience in a wide range of practices, including emerging practices, and practices in related disciplines that may not, at first glance, seem likely to fit conventional ideas of practice. In addition, the handbook points you to professional organizations in other countries so that you can begin to find out for yourself what the options for experience abroad might be.

The internship year or professional experience year is the first time most undergraduate architecture students spend a significant period in professional architectural or related employment. It is often the first stepping stone in a long career, and is therefore an important one. The right choice at the beginning will allow you to establish a direction for your professional career, and will advance and support your education. The right choice may also open doors you have not imagined, and change the way you think about the design and production of space, from buildings, cities, landscapes, and regions right down to designed objects and virtual environments. It may well impact your choice of graduate study, and beyond. We hope that this book will help to guide you through many of the choices you will need to make as you consider where and how to apply for a position, how to interview, how to be a productive member of an office, and how to make sure that you get as many elements of the experience you need to eventually get licensed or registered as an architect.

The main thing to remember as you read the book is that architectural offices vary enormously in the work they do and the way they treat their employees. Offices can also change with time. Licensing laws and professional charters can change too. We offer you a lot of advice. However, we also strongly advise you to check everything said here with advice from different licensing institutions in different countries and the expectations of individual offices. Nonetheless, if you follow the guidance in this book, and if you add your own intelligent research, this book should support you to make better choices and, more importantly, to have more choices to make in the first place.

The handbook consists of 13 chapters and two appendices at the end listing resources where you can go for more information. It explains the main ways to get the professional experience you need to get licensed or registered in the UK or the USA. We touch on a few variations in the process to show that the relationship between professional experience, education and licensing or registration as an architect varies in different countries as well as within the two countries that form the main focus of the handbook, the UK and the USA.

In Chapter 1, *Practicing in the Built Environment*, we introduce you to the notion of an architectural office and some key terms you might encounter in practice.

In Chapter 2, *The Architectural Office*, we elaborate further on the characteristics of an office, discussing the main types of practice you should consider within the architectural profession.

In Chapter 3, *Other Types of Office,* we introduce other types of practice in the built environment, from interior design and construction to landscape architecture and engineering.

In Chapter 4, *Critical and Emerging Practices*, we look at alternative forms of practice – the types of architectural and other practice that may not, at first glance, fit the expectations of internship or professional experience at all. We outline the ideas of theorists who have written about critical practice and how to think differently about professional education and professional organizations. We show how some of these ideas explain the recent emergence of critical practices in architecture and why this is an important development for the architectural profession.

In Chapter 5, *The Year Out and Beyond*, we describe professional experience and the process of becoming an architect in the UK. We outline the expectation for the professional experience period, and explain how the different stages of taking professional examinations relate to professional experience in practice.

In Chapter 6, *Internship and Beyond*, we describe professional experience and the process of becoming an architect in the USA. We explain how the Internship Development Program (IDP) in the USA works, the expectations of both student and employer, and the different ways in which professional experience and architectural education combine to lead up to the Architectural Registration Examination (ARE).

In Chapter 7, *International Experience*, we discuss different ways of becoming an architect in other countries, how to look for a job abroad, and some of the main opportunities and limitations.

In Chapters 8–10, respectively, *UK, USA, and Other International Case Studies*, we introduce a variety of design practices to show how professional experience differs, yet also has much in common, across the world. In order to emphasize differences and similarities among different practices, the firms are presented in a case study format.

In Chapter 11, *Finding a Job*, we describe some ways of finding and getting the right job. We talk about how to present yourself and your work through your application letter and portfolio, follow-up contacts, the interview and any subsequent negotiations. We make suggestions about what you should expect as a year-out student or intern, and different employment formats and contracts, including variations in benefits.

In Chapter 12, *Office Cultures*, we outline basic expectations of professional behaviour once you are employed. We cover subjects such as dress code, punctuality, time management, gender, race and sexuality at the office, professional ethics, dealing with clients, community service, socializing with the office, and handling conflicts.

Finally, in Chapter 13, *Afterwards*, we discuss how to terminate your employment, how to survive termination, how to stay on good terms with former employers, how to move on to the next position, or graduate school, or related fields of practice. We talk briefly about career options after taking the final professional or licensing examination, and how to use your architectural experience when making major career changes. We conclude this chapter and the book by advising you how to use your professional experience to in turn become a good mentor to interns and year-out students yourself.

Appendix A is a bibliography of useful readings about professional experience. Appendix B contains a list of nearly 100 web sites where you can find information about international architectural practice and experience in related practice areas.

In short, this handbook, describes many of the key issues you need to know about when you begin your first experience of practice in architecture. If you use the handbook well, it should help you decide where you want to be heading, how you can find and keep a position that advances your education and career, and what kind of employment is appropriate as a first step on your long journey to becoming a competent and committed professional.

SECTION ONE: WHERE TO GO

# 1 Practicing in the Built Environment

Most internship programmes require interns to acquire experience under the direct supervision of a registered architect. Before going into greater detail about the nature of this supervision, it is important to understand that the work of architecture can take many different forms and lead you to a number of different professional destinations. In a global market the work of architecture is becoming increasingly diverse, bringing together architects and other allied design professionals. It is precisely because of this practical diversity that it is very hard to categorize contemporary architectural practices, but for the purposes of this handbook we will outline some examples. This chapter contains such examples. These have been selected from a wide range of professional destinations in contemporary architectural practice as well as other practices in related disciplines in the built environment and the arts. They outline the kind of destinations where it may be possible for you to gain internship credit (USA) or experience you can include on your Professional Experience and Development Record (UK). We hope that this will allow you to think more broadly about your interests, and the areas of practice from which you will be able to learn, and in which you may wish to work.

Before you begin to think about the kind of experience you may want or need, you should be aware that in general the requirements of professional training, including those in the USA and in the UK, can cover a wide range of expertise in various categories and that sometimes you might need to work in several offices in order to fulfil all of them. Also, please note that if you are working under the supervision of a registered landscape architect, engineer or other professional, or in a firm whose practice does not encompass the comprehensive range of architectural practice, your maximum training units or internship credits allowed might be limited. Some offices may offer elements of experience that will not provide training units or internship credits at all, but you may wish to gain experience there in order to better prepare you for the next job that can contribute towards credits or units.

In outlining the kind of practices suitable for a part or all of your year out or internship year, we also urge you to check regularly for any updates or changes in the internship legislation or year-out requirements of your country. You will need to contact the professional licensing organization appropriate to your situation (Architects' Registration Board (ARB) and Royal Institute of British Architects (RIBA) in the UK, National Council of Architectural Registration Boards (NCARB) for the USA), read the information you are given very carefully, usually make telephone calls if anything in unclear, and enlist the help and advice of other professionals as well if some of the process still appears mysterious or confusing. At the end of this book we provide a list of web sites for professional architectural organizations in many countries across the world to allow you to access as much information and key individuals as quickly as possible. Remember, when in doubt, ask, and if still unclear, ask again. You do not want to work for months and find that the time you have spent working will not count towards licensing (unless, of course, you love the work for its own sake).

## The Architectural Office

The first decision you will need to make when planning your professional experience year is in which kind of office you are going to be looking for work. If the economy is good, and you are a good student, and also ideally already have a little experience, you may have a fair amount of choice. You may consider working in an engineering, construction, landscape, urban planning or interior design practice, but your choice will most likely first include an architectural office.

An architectural office – one of the most common destinations, and historically the greatest magnet for recent graduates – is a loose common name for wide range practices that vary in size, scope of work, expertise, and location. The design and construction of buildings is a complex process and involves many steps. As an intern in an architectural office you will work under the supervision of a more experienced architect and will most likely have the opportunity to be involved in schematic design, design development, construction documents, construction administration, site inspection and so on. NCARB in the USA defines 16 areas of competency, raging from project programming to community and professional service and it can be a challenge to plug in your experience on a particular project into an appropriate category. To help you make decisions about how best to organize your practical experience, you should always discuss the progress of your internship year or year out with your supervisor, mentor, and other interns, so as to define how various project phases fit into the training area descriptions. You should also make sure that you understand clearly the expectations of your supervisor and mentor (see Chapter 5: UK and Chapter 6: USA, for detailed information), and how they might help you to get a broader spread of architectural experience. Your mentor should act as a guide not only to the experience you will get, but can also help you make choices about where to focus your job applications. Although a mentor is not always perfect, she/he can also help you to present your existing skills and assets so as to have a good chance of getting the job you want and help you understand why certain skills are essential to success and how they fit the professional architectural world. If you need to read more about architectural practice, a list of general readings is included in Appendix A.

## Computer-Aided Design and Digital Skills

Whereas the industrial revolution provided a context for architectural production based on physical proximity between users, designers, and sites of production and construction, this condition is now changing. Digital practices are becoming the nucleus of a virtual workplace; physical proximity is becoming less critical and a global distribution of production is becoming more and more normal. The ability to post your files online and send them through e-mail has contributed enormously to the globalization of architectural practices. Glass panels for a building may be produced in Mexico from construction packages digitally created jointly between a design team in New York and a construction documentation team located in India or Russia, then may be sent to California or Singapore for finishing and finally be delivered and assembled as part of a building in France or Australia. One might work in London on an urban project in China, while at the same time designing a web site that facilitates communication among clients, designers, contractors, and other parties involved to which construction drawings, specifications, memos, and other information is submitted, and which therefore becomes a kind of virtual office. For some of these terms (e.g. construction drawings, specifications) see the section on common terms below.

The global production, transportation, and assembly of architectural products means that it is less likely that you will be able to visit the factory workshop of the subcontractor or supplier involved in the construction of your project, and more likely that you will be working through digitally produced norms. The consultants may meet a few times at a major urban centre to coordinate face to face, but the rest of the communication process may remain entirely virtual.

Even if the majority of offices have only partially virtual practices, there are few offices that have not been impacted by digital technology. It is therefore essential for interns to develop a sense of comfort within the digital environment. Whichever architectural office becomes the destination for your year out or internship year, you can be almost certain of one thing. You will need to have at least basic skills in AutoCAD or MicroStation. Computer-aided design (CAD) skills are essential to getting and keeping a job in nearly all offices. While there are still offices that do drawings by hand, they are rare, and becoming rarer every day. If you do not have CAD skills, you need to find a way to teach yourself or take classes. If your school of architecture does not offer CAD classes (and some do not, because learning CAD essentially involves mechanical learning), get together with fellow students who know the rudiments, or take an evening class and begin learning. Once you begin, you will find your skills evolve quickly as you are asked to do more and more, whether at school or at the office. It is also helpful, though it can be expensive, if you purchase the latest version of the CAD system of your choice, and update it as new versions are issued, so that you are up to date and competitive in the job marketplace. You may, however, sometimes find that your office may not have the most up to date version. If you find that comfort with digital technology grows into a digital passion, you should consider applying to those offices that are leaders in the application of new technologies in design, representation, manufacturing, and construction. These are discussed in greater detail in Chapter 4.

Resources

Szalapaj, P., *CAD Principles for Architectural Design* (Oxford: Architectural Press, 2001)
Snyder, J., *Architectural Construction Drawings with AutoCAD R14* (New York: James Wiley, 1998)

## Some Common Terms

We would like to introduce you to some key terms you may encounter in an architectural office, and may not at first know what these mean. Knowing these may give you a much better idea of what kind of work you might be doing in the office, and may help you make the right decision about a job. The examples below form just a small selection, and you should check any terms you do not understand with your mentor as well as other students who are working in similar context and in the same country, as terms can have different meanings in different contexts. For more information, see the end of this section.

### Construction Drawings and Documents

The term construction drawing sounds very clear, but construction drawings, their content, and sequence of production can vary from office to office and certainly vary from country to country. Construction drawings are drawings that contain information that is necessary for a building to be built. They can include site drawings with soil information, topographic detail and landscape treatment, structural drawings showing foundations and superstructure, masonry, carpentry, electrical and mechanical services drawings, detail drawings including cabinetry, decorations, and schedules including plumbing and electrical fittings, ironmongery, and so on. On a large job construction drawings can number thousands, and for larger jobs are generally organized into packages so that they are easy to separate and price by different building trades. Construction drawings form a part of construction documents – the document package that in turn forms the building contract. This includes among other items the construction drawings, but also specifications and the list of activities for the project from start to finish.

It is important for you to know that you will get construction drawing experience, as that is the stage of building production when you learn the most about how design affects and is affected by materials, components, systems, and processes. However, you should ask as many questions as possible about the kind of construction drawings you may be asked to do. For example, if you are asked to be a part of a team producing 50% construction drawings, that means that you will only be involved in schematic construction, and the actual construction drawings will be done by the architect of record (in the USA, this is an architect licensed by the state in which the project is due to be built). You may therefore not get the full construction drawing experience you need. Sometimes students are asked to get involved in only one part of a construction drawing set, particularly if the project is a large one. Try to avoid that situation if you can – your success during your year out or internship year relies on you being able to get as broad and integrated a professional experience as you can. If the commitment from the office is only to certain construction drawing packages (see below), and you have the choice of another job with broader experience, you may wish to walk away from the overly narrow focus unless you really want to build up deeper expertise in that area and are willing to wait a bit longer to get licensed.

## Gross-to-Net Ratio

Another term you may encounter in a larger office is "gross-to-net ratio". This is the formula used to calculate the efficiency and profitability of buildings available for rental or leasing, particularly commercial buildings. The gross-to-net ratio is the ratio of actual lettable space (measured from the inside of the exterior wall, not including communal circulation space, toilets and service zones, including lifts or elevators and staircases) to the gross area (the total area of the building, including all of the above plus the exterior walls). The closer the gross-to-net ratio, the more efficient and more profitable the building. In larger offices that specialize in commercial buildings you will come across expert designers who know how to do this. Such designers are highly sought by commercial clients, though being able to maximize profit may not always lead to the most meaningful design. As with many other areas of specialization, here you need to decide if this is the kind of experience you want, and whether you will get a broad range of other jobs to do in the office as well.

## Packages

You may be asked to be responsible for a "package" of drawings, such as a cladding package. This means you will need to produce a drawing set containing all information needed to manufacture and install cladding in the project. You may well have to produce such a package before the rest of the construction drawings are complete, as more and more building projects these days are run on a tight time line, and drawing packages are staggered so that the materials are priced, manufactured and arrive on site just in time for that part of the job – not too soon, and not too late. This saves the client and contractor a great deal of money, as fee, material, production and construction costs need be paid only when they are needed. Packages may also be used if a project is to be built in phases, and in the USA the term package can be used to refer to an entire job contract. Packages can be a problem if you work on one package for months and it only contains work relating to one trade. If you are offered 6 months of doing the package for service catwalks above a suspended ceiling, and you are not desperate for money, do not take the job. It will not get you much year-out/internship credit, and will challenge only your patience, not other skills that you already have.

## Punch or Snagging List

The snagging list in the UK and the punch list in the USA are both important terms, as they both signal the end of a project. They are both lists of work that needs to be done for a building project to reach final completion. In different countries the punch or snagging list has different time lines, and different amounts of money are held back by the client until the work is done; but essentially until the items on the list are done, final completion cannot take place. If an office offers you a position that will take you right to the punch or snagging list phase, you know you will see the job through to the end. The punch or snagging lists will need your full attention, as once work on a snagging or punch list is completed, you usually cannot ask a contractor to come back and do work that was not on the list simply because you or the client forgot to include it (unless, of course, it was a defect covered by the contract or subcontracts and their various warranties). Examples of work on such list might be dents in plasterwork that need to be filled, missing ironmongery (UK term, called hardware in the USA) that needs to be fitted, unbalanced heating systems that require adjustment, flaws in glazing, planting that died during construction due to contractor neglect, and so on. These days standard punch or snagging lists are available through software systems, so you do not start from scratch. Regardless of the way your list is generated, keeping a close eye on cumulative list of incomplete work by an architectural team, and working closely with your client during this phase is the secret to a good punch or snagging list.

## Shop Drawings

Shop drawings are construction drawings produced not by the architect, but by the manufacturer, subcontractor, or supplier. They can also be called the erection plans or framing plans, and are used to fabricate a product that includes all dimensions, materials, tolerances, etc. Typical shop drawings are steel or cabinetry drawings. The task of the architect, often together with key consultants (the structural engineer for steelwork drawings, and the interior designer for cabinetry drawings), is to check these to make sure that materials, assembly and dimensions are correct. This is a very exacting task, and if done badly, can create major cost headaches and lead to frustrated contractors and consultants as well as clients. If you find that you are interviewing for a position that involves you checking shop drawings, always ask to work with a more experienced person in the office who can guide you and provide a safety-net by double checking on critical elements of the process. In a one-person practice always ask the principal of the practice to do so – you do not want to be solely responsible for any part of the construction process. On a positive front, shop drawings are a great way to understand how suppliers and consultants communicate, and precisely how building components are made, but checking them can be very complex, and require real concentration. If it is nearby, you might ask the office to take you to the suppliers or fabricator's factory so that you can see how they make the materials you will be checking, and why they need the information in a particular format. Understanding the actual physical process can be incredibly helpful. Of course if the steelwork for your job is being made in Korea and you are in Canada, that option may not open to you, but in general, seeing the workshop or factory will not only really expand your understanding of the process, but will help build a really good relationship with your fabricator or supplier. Such relationships can be extremely helpful in designing and constructing good buildings.

### Specifications

You may be asked to be a part of a specification writing team. Specification writing is not a job usually given to year-out students or interns by themselves, as it is a critical legal part of a project and needs to be 100% accurate. A specification consists of an accurate and detailed description of each material, element, fitting or process in a building, and includes references to legislatively or institutionally approved norms and processes for making and installing building parts, including materials, components and assemblies. Specification writing is a specialist field in itself, and if you are asked to take part in this, make sure that you are working under the supervision of a senior person in your office. As with checking shop drawings, you will need to enjoy methodical, precise work. A slight error in a specification may have dramatic impact – for example if an error in specifying the strength of steel in a project occurs, the health and safety of your client and all the subsequent users of a building may be involved. If you get involved in a specification writing team, always, always ask if you are unsure of anything.

### Turnkey Project

The term turnkey refers to the turning of the key when a client walks into a completed building and represents a design and construction service that begins with a feasibility study and end with a complete building, including the supply of furniture, furnishings, equipment, and sometimes material supplies, maintenance personnel, marketing, etc. It is the most complete service a firm can provide for a client and usually involves many more consultants than a traditional architectural project, from financial and real estate advice at the beginning, to managerial and janitorial expertise at the end. A turnkey project will give you a tremendous depth of knowledge about how buildings work, but parts of the process will not count towards your practical experience credits, so make sure you ask exactly what your role on a project of this kind would be, and check this with your mentor. Depending on the type of project it may also take some time, perhaps longer than the year or so you wish to spend in an architectural office. Turnkey projects are more common in civil and structural engineering companies than in architectural offices.

## Resources

Philbin, T., *The Illustrated Dictionary of Building Terms* (McGraw Hill Professional, 1996)
*AIA East Tennessee Glossary of Architectural and Construction Terms*: www.aiaetn.org/glossary.html
*Hancock Joist, Joist and Structural Glossary*: www.hancockjoist.com/glossary.htm
Styles, K., *Working Drawings Handbook* (Oxford: Architectural Press, 1995)
Huth, M. and Wells, W., *Understanding Construction Drawings*, Delmar Learning, 1999
Enwright Associates, Inc. (for gross-to-net ratios): www.enwright.com/Resource_Center/Ratios/corporate.html
Rosen, H.J., *Construction Specification Writing* (New York: John Wiley and Sons, 1998)

# 2   The Architectural Office

Offices may have very different approaches to design and deal only with specific issues, or specialize in a particular building type. Often offices use the word "fit" when asked why they hired or did not hire a particular employee. The word fit really means whether there is a match between the attitude and design approach of the job applicant, and the office culture and design approach of an office. No architectural office is exactly like another and therefore below we outline the differences between some of the most common types of approach in architectural practice.

## Office Types

### The Large Office

The most important difference in the nature of experience in architectural offices most often relates to the size of the firm. Some offices have more than 300 employees, a few have thousands of employees, with offices across the globe, while others can have less than ten. And, in the USA and the UK at least, nearly 50% of offices consist of solo practitioners – men and women often working from a front room or a garage in their home, on small jobs, usually renovations or re-modelling projects. Recently an additional office type, the boutique firm, has joined the two other types. The boutique firm is a small office that often focuses only on one or two building types, say private homes or small retail stores, and builds up such a reputation that it can be selective about work. All types of office can provide excellent experience, but you need to know the difference between them. The question you therefore need to ask first is – would you like join a large and complex corporate environment, a small specialized setting, or are you more comfortable doing a wide range of tasks with perhaps only one other person?

Large offices can offer you a range of projects, typically big in scale, and they might also give you an opportunity to work on projects around the world. Sometimes larger offices might be divided into smaller studios, covering different market or building types, others may cover a variety of related disciplines. The largest firm in the world is Gensler, with offices in many major cities in the USA, and projects spanning a broad range of design services in numerous global locations. Perhaps the most well-known of the large firms, with offices around the world, is Skidmore Owings and Merrill (SOM), sometimes affectionately called "SOM University" because of the number of interns it has hired, many of whom have gone on to become outstanding practitioners and educators. SOM, like a number of large firms with globally significant projects, combines many disciplines related to architecture in one firm, such as engineering, urban planning, interior design, and so on. It has different divisions, including those that specialize in high-rise (called "supertall") buildings, urban and regional planning, project management and graphic design. SOM has offices in major US cities, as well as in London, Shanghai, and Hong Kong. This means that if you stay there, in the longer term you might get the opportunity to work in a number of different areas of expertise and may gain experience in one of its offices abroad.

The likelihood of real choices in types of work when working for a large firm allows you the possibility to both rise and move across in the firm into areas best suited to your talents. You should remember that once you are hired into an area, an office begins to invest in your skills there, so moving across into another section may not be as easy once you are past the beginner stage. Another large firm, O'Donnell Wicklund Pigozzi and Petersen (OWP&P, see Chapter 9, Case Studies), has a portfolio of work that covers a broad range of specializations from school design to senior housing, from feasibility studies and retail design. It too has work abroad, but being smaller, the opportunity to do this would not be as frequent as at a very large firm such as SOM. Being smaller, and having begun as a suburban firm, it is able to treat its 300 employees more like a large family. Duffy Eley Giffone Worthington, in the UK, is a large firm that has made a very strong name for itself for its in-depth expertise in designing space and providing expertise in the management strategy for large, usually commercial clients looking to be innovative in their organizational structures. Another large UK office,

Foster Associates, specializes in high-tech design (see below and Chapter 6, for more detail). Finally, there are large offices in many countries across the world. Your national professional architectural organization should be able to refer you to magazine articles or its own records for a list of such offices.

The drawback of a large firm, and this varies from firm to firm, and of course also depends on the state of the economy, is that you may end up working on a particular segment of a project for a long time. If this starts to cause any anxiety for you, share your concerns with your supervisor and see if you can be assigned to a different type of project phase – to doing some contract administration, or going to client meetings for the planning phase of another project. Having said that, bear in mind that some phases might require more substantial experience, and it might be a while until you are permitted or able to comfortably perform in all of the aspects of an architectural project. In fact you may not be able to get the whole range of experience in one firm.

In a large office you may also find a more competitive environment but at the top of the ladder the salaries can be very high indeed. If money is important to you, you are more likely to earn a high salary at the top of the management pyramid of a large office than in a small one.

Large offices also can have very particular cultures. Some have a dress code (no jeans, etc.) and might be more formal than smaller offices in their expectation of your attendance. It is helpful to find out as much about the formal as well as informal culture of a large office from other students who work there so you can decide whether you might enjoy that world or not before you apply. It is helpful to check the office's commitment to diversity as well – find out how many partners and associates are female and/or persons colour. Corporate culture exists to create solidarity and a coherent set of practices in a large organization, to offer a broad range of services and expertise in large projects. A large office can offer you opportunities that you may not be able to find elsewhere – you may end up doing projects overseas, may get to know and work with leading consultants, learn to be part of and manage teams, and be able to specialize in some unusual areas.

Some Large Offices

- Gensler: www.gensler.com
- Skidmore Owings and Merrill: www.som.com
- O'Donnell Wicklund Pigozzi and Peterson: www.owpp.com
- Duffy Eley Giffone Worthington: www.degw.com

## The Small Office

Smaller firms can give you an opportunity to be involved in a greater range of project phases, including construction administration. Often you can get very good experience in a very small, one- or two-person firm, because you will do a little (or a lot) of everything. You may end up not only doing design and construction drawings, and participating in site inspections or supervision, but may also get involved in programming projects in the office, handling budgets, coordinating consultants, going to client meetings, handling contract and legislative issues, preparing marketing materials, and so on. In some small firms you may get very high-quality experience indeed. You will most likely have to follow the architectural approach of the firm very closely, but if the firm has been able to be selective about the jobs that it takes on, you may get a very high level of design experience, with follow-through in all phases of a project. Wheeler Kearns Architects (see Chapter 9, Case Studies) is one example of a small firm that focuses primarily on private homes for discerning clients, and gives significant responsibility to its employees. Everyone, from the partners to the intern, makes coffee and files product materials, and the office is run as a cooperative. High-quality design work and democratic policies make this kind of firm very desirable as a workplace and such offices have to turn down many applications from interns.

The drawback of a small firm is that you may not have a large circle of experts to help advise you about a problem, may get involved in more crisis management due to the tightness of architectural fees, may have higher stress levels due to the short duration of projects, and could well be looking after the office when your boss goes on holiday. The culture in a small office will often be set by your boss and if there is a mismatch between you and that person, your diplomatic skills may be tested, but at the same time may benefit from being developed and honed. Boyarsky Murphy, Yrki and Testbedstudio (see Case Studies in Chapters 8–10) are other small firms that do very good work and give responsibility to their employees, but like Wheeler Kearns above, get many more applications than they have opportunities. Do not dismiss a firm, because it is small, and certainly do not dismiss it if it is not well known. Experience in a small firm can be very rewarding and a great stepping stone to more experience, including setting up your own firm.

### Some Small Offices

* Boyarsky Murphy, London, UK: www.boyarskymurphy.com
* Testbedstudio, Malmö, Sweden: www.testbedstudio.com

- Wheeler Kearns Architects, Chicago, IL, USA: www.wkarch.com
- Yrki, Reykjavik, Iceland: www.ai.is/e-ai.htm

## Offices and Building Types

If you have an interest in offices that handle specific building types, you should do additional research and look for those offices that fit your ambitions. Although offices increasingly undertake a broad range of building types to cover themselves in case there is a downturn in one area of specialization, there are still offices that carry in-house skills in specific building types. Such specializations may include retail facilities, office buildings, transportations facilities (airports and bus terminals, railway stations, etc.), and so on. For example, Santiago Calatrava has developed a very strong reputation for designing railway/mass transit stations, and SOM are one of the world leaders in high-rise office buildings.

Hospitals and research laboratories form another specialization in building type. They involve close collaboration with medical and technical specialists. They tend to be designed by specialized firms, and involve a lot of collaboration with mechanical and other services engineers due to the complexity of materials used, the safety standards involved, and the legal liabilities involved if you make a mistake. You may end up designing lead-lined rooms to house magnetic resonance imaging machines, special laboratory airlocks to protect unique strains of genetically engineered mice and transparent waste systems carrying waste laboratory materials. If you are fascinated by science, then this may be the internship for you, but here too you will need to demonstrate your commitment, experience if you have some, and reliability.

To get involved in a private house design you are more likely to have to look for a mid-size or a smaller boutique firm. Large offices do not normally take on house commissions, unless it is for a client who already has a larger project in the office. Some firms that have designed outstanding private homes are Wheeler Kearns Architects and Richard Meier Architects.

If your diploma or a thesis project covered a particular building type that you would like to research further, make sure that your portfolio clearly demonstrates that interest. It may be helpful to collect magazine articles, surf the web, and try to get information via the student grapevine as to which offices currently have, or may soon have projects in your area of interest. If a firm does not have current work, but has strengths in your area of interest, send a résumé and portfolio anyway, and then call regularly to check if an appropriate project has arrived.

If this is really important to you, you can do so even if you have found another position, though you would have to make sure that you have a definite job offer before giving the required period of notice at your present firm.

Offices are becoming more and more diverse in their projects in order to shield themselves against an economic downturn in a particular market sector, so you need to connect to your personal information grapevine (other students, professors, architectural magazines) to check which firms have some degree of specialization in building type. Professional architectural organizations in your country may be a useful source of information about specializations as well.

Resources

•  Santiago Calatrava: www.calatrava.com
•  Medical Architecture Research Unit: www.lsbu.ac.uk/maru/
•  YRM Architects Designers Planners: www.yrm.co.uk
•  Skidmore Owings and Merrill: www.som.com
•  O'Donnell Wicklund Pigozzi and Peterson: www.owpp.com
•  Wheeler Kearns Architects: www.wkarch.com
•  Richard Meier Architects: www.richardmeier.com

## Other Kinds of Architectural Office

Whereas a broad range of building types in an office's portfolio is becoming more normal, a broad range of design approaches is not. Some offices maintain diverse stylistic, philosophical or theoretical responses within the same firm, but this is rare, because on the whole an office often needs to be identified with a unique kind of service, and a particular aesthetic in order to market itself to clients. We have outlined some, but not all of these different technical, formal, and theoretical approaches below, in alphabetical order. In Chapters 8–10 you will find more information – numerous case studies of architectural offices, many of which have areas of specialization – either in building type or in design approach.

### The Community Practice

Working in the area of community architecture, you will learn that the environment is not only physical and legislative, but is also social, defined by local culture, neighbourhood, and various communities.

You will become involved in the processes through which a community learns to understand, represent and change their spatial and cultural expectations, works with architects to produce feasibility studies allowing the client to go out and look for funds to build a project. In a job like this you may learn to help plan meetings, carefully consider input from various audiences, such as community groups or historic preservation organizations, present proposals to many constituencies, and sometimes handle major differences in opinion among your clients. You will learn to work to a budget, and in some instances may not get paid as much, or much at all. The Rural Studio, for example, has an outreach programme that invites students and fellows from around the world to participate in the programme. These participants do not get professional intern credits. If your school of architecture has a teaching unit that handles community architecture, it can be very helpful if you get experience there, as that will give you an advantage when you look for a job in that kind of organization. This kind of work is not always architecturally glamorous, but it can be one of the most meaningful things you will do in your life.

## Resources

- Matrix Architects, UK: www.matrixarchitects.com
- APSR (Architects and Planners for Social Responsibility): www.adpsr.org
- City Design Center, University of Illinois at Chicago, USA: www.uic.edu/aa/cdc/
- The Rural Studio, Alabama, USA: www.ruralstudio.com

### *The Conservation or Historic Preservation Office*

A practice specializing in conservation, or historic preservation of buildings has specific expertise in architectural, construction and often also social history, as well as access to very specific expertise related to particular building materials and construction methods. In such an office you will learn where to go for important archival material, and will most likely learn how to do very careful survey or measured drawings. Offices of this kind do not usually make a great deal of money as historic preservation or conservation in most countries does not take preference over new build, and offices involved in this kind of work usually work for dedicated but not well-funded organizations. However, if you have an interest in traditional construction, have researched the history of the area where you wish to live or work, love to work with craftsmen, enjoy doing measured drawings, like to sit in archives doing research, then this is the job for you. Historic preservation can also include modernist buildings. Historic preservation and conservation are much more prominent as types of practice in Europe; but if you are interested in doing this kind of work in other locations, local architectural organizations should be able to point you in the right direction. Voluntary Service Overseas in the UK sometimes gets involved in preservation projects abroad, as can the Peace Corps in USA. UNESCO World Heritage sites are another useful starting point as many of these sites do not have the full funding necessary for their preservation and may be looking for volunteers. The National Trust in the UK and in the USA should be able to give you useful contacts to pursue your interests further, as should a number of other organizations dedicated to preserving historical heritage, such as DoCoMoMo, or the Association for Industrial Archaeology in the UK, called the Society for Industrial Archaeology in the USA, as well as local historical societies. There are numerous smaller organizations in the UK dedicated to historic preservation, ranging from the British Toilet Association, advocating for the retention and improvement of public toilets, to Subterranea Britannica, dedicated to the understanding and preservation of man-made underground places. The web site of the *Journal of Architectural Conservation* hosts an excellent book list on historic preservation.

There is also another kind of conservation practice. If buildings have not been properly designed in the first place, building failures can begin to occur. Although to some degree every architectural office does this every day, there are specialist firms who understand materials and construction to such a fine degree of detail that they can diagnose a building problem and offer lasting solutions. Working in this area confronts you with the imperfections of the profession, but it is very valuable, as it may make the difference between saving or losing a good building, and may make life much better for the building's users. In many cases the building may not be of historic, but may of tremendous functional value. One firm that specializes in this area is Bickerdike Allen Partners in the UK, which consists of architects who also have expertise in specific types of building construction and materials. If you love learning about building materials and construction, if you love imagining and solving disaster scenarios, if you are methodical and like working in a team that may involve materials research scientists, engineers, soil scientists, and so on, this could be the job for you.

Resources

Fielden, B., Sir, *Conservation of Historic Buildings* (Oxford: Architectural Press, 2003)
Maddox, D. (ed.), *All About Old Buildings*, National Trust for Historic Preservation (Washington, DC: Preservation Press, 1985)
*Journal of Architectural Conservation*: www.donhead.com/Journal%20of%20Architectural%20Conservation.htm
*Journal of Architectural Conservation* book list page: www.donhead.com/Book%20List.htm

Professional Associations

- National Trust, UK: www.nationaltrust.org.uk/environment
- National Trust for Historic Preservation, USA: www.nationaltrust.org
- DoCoMoMo: www.docomomo-us.org
- English Heritage: www.english-heritage.org.uk
- The Society for Industrial Archaeology, USA: www.social.mtu.edu/IA/sia.html
- The Association for Industrial Archaeology, UK: www.industrial-archaeology.org.uk
- British Toilet Association: www.britloos.co.uk
- Subterranea Britannica: www.subbrit.org.uk

Practices

- Bickerdike Allen Partners, London, UK: www.bickerdikeallen.com
- Julian Harrap Architects, London, UK: www.julianharraparchitects.co.uk
- Simpson and Brown Architects, Edinburgh, UK: www.simpsonandbrown.co.uk

## The High-Tech Practice

Another type of design approach is that of the high-tech office. High-tech offices generally employ industrial and post-industrial technologies, both as a visual symbol and as inherent content of building design. High-tech buildings tend to serve building programmes with a technical component, or building programmes that need to be symbolically perceived as progressive and technical in emphasis. Examples of high-tech building can therefore include broadcasting companies, hospitals, computer chip factories, and even corporate headquarters. Often the construction detail of high-tech buildings is carefully designed and machined, and emphasizes mechanistic forms, especially in the detail. Sometimes the details can be true works of art, and ironically involve an initially high level of craft. High-tech buildings can also include significant use of digital or environmental technology.

High-tech is particularly popular in the UK, with firms like Foster Associates, Wilkinson Eyre, the Richard Rogers Partnership, and Grimshaw Architects standing as good examples. In the USA, Murphy Jahn and in Germany, Günter Behnisch form other good examples of architectural offices that integrate and symbolize advanced technological thinking through architectural design. The Lloyd's building in London, UK, or the Centre Pompidou in Paris are both examples of high-tech architecture, where the building main design content consists of the expression of its mechanical, structural, and circulation systems, and is built from materials requiring sophisticated contemporary manufacturing methods. Working on such buildings can take a great deal of time, as great attention is given to detail design, much of it a process of creating one-off elements, requiring the making of prototypes before the actual building components can be made. The Lloyd's building, for example, had thousands of construction drawings for that very reason. If you end up working for a high-tech practice you can expect to do much more detailed design, sometimes involving specialist consultants and manufacturers, making maquettes, carving prototypes in wood or casting them in wax or plaster in preparation for manufacture. You will most likely also learn a great deal about heating, ventilation, and air conditioning systems, and how to turn these into an expressive element of design. If you love that degree of detail, are fascinated by building systems and love steel, glass, cable, and high-tech fabrics, then this kind of job should be right for you. Again, as with all other specializations, the more design work and research in this area you have in your portfolio, the more commitment and experience you will be able to show in your application.

## Some High-Tech Firms

- Foster Associates, London, UK: www.foster-fa.com
- The Richard Rogers Partnership, London, UK: www.richardrogers.co.uk
- Wilkinson Eyre, London, UK: www.wilkinsoneyre.com
- Grimshaw Architects, London, UK: www.grimshaw-architects.com
- Eva Jiricna Architects, London, UK and Czech Republic: http://www.ejal.com/

- Behnisch, Behnisch, and Partner, Stuttgart, Germany, EU, and Los Angeles, USA: www.behnisch.com
- Murphy Jahn, Chicago, IL: www.murphyjahn.com

## The Historicist Practice

Given the roots of much of European and North American architecture in the classical tradition, and after architectural postmodernism rejected modernist architecture, neo-classical buildings have been making a comeback both in the UK and in the USA. While the design of some of these buildings has been as superficial as the Dryvit or drywall from which these buildings are made, some architectural practices have seriously researched traditional architecture and construction, and feel strongly that this is the best way to design. In such practices you would most likely learn the classical orders, design according to classical proportional systems, study classicism during different historical periods, learn how to do measured drawings, and work with suppliers who are expert in working in this kind of aesthetic. You may, however, have to do some of the learning in your own time, as architectural fees in your practice may not be high enough to support the cost of that time.

A firm may not limit itself to one historical period, although many do. Some firms believe that the use of an appropriate historical style needs to emerge from the needs of the client and the characteristics of the site, and may therefore draw on historical knowledge from many periods. Whilst this might be seen as eclectic, the firms who are outstanding in this type of work usually have partners or principals who have a deep knowledge of architectural history, not only from a stylistic but also from a social and cultural point of view, and you can learn a great deal about the relationship between aesthetics, form, materials, construction, and social ritual in different periods. If research into historical periods is your passion, then the more study you do on your own or in classes before you seek work, the stronger your chances of getting a position would be. Both the UK and the USA have some well-known architectural offices specializing in historic styles, as well as architecture schools that will introduce you to this body of knowledge.

Resource

Long, H., *Victorian Houses and Their Details* (Oxford: Architectural Press, 2002) see also Resources for Conservation/Historic Preservation Practice

Some Historicist Firms

- Robert Adam Architects, London and Winchester, UK: www.robertadamarchitects.com
- Cohen and Hacker Architects, Evanston, Illinois, USA: www.cohen-hacker.com
- John Simpson and Partners, London, UK: www.johnsimpsonarchitects.com
- Thomas Gordon Smith Architects, South Bend, Indiana, USA: www.thomasgordonsmitharchitects.com

Professional and Educational Institutions

- The Prince's Foundation, UK: www.princes-foundation.org
- School of Architecture, University of Notre Dame, USA: www.nd.edu/~arch/\
- The Institute of Classical Architecture and Classical America: www.classicist.org

## The Minimalist Practice

Minimalist architecture has become very popular since the rise and fall of postmodernism. Minimalist architects specialize in the design of spaces with clear and simple spatial articulation, the minimum amount of detail and careful detailing of a small range of materials in a single project. Influenced by minimalist art, and like modernist architects, minimalists rely heavily on shaping the quality of light, and abstracting form to its essentials. Minimalist architects often use a broader, and at times more expensive range of materials than modernists. Many minimalist practices design buildings and interiors for clients with a great deal of wealth and taste, as minimalist building components are not available off the shelf, and so have to be specially designed and fabricated.

The office of John Pawson forms perhaps the clearest example of minimalism, and John Pawson has himself produced a book about this style. The Swiss practice Herzog de Meuron can also be described as minimalists. However, it can also incorporate iconographic elements into the office's work, which act almost as a Pop Art influence, such as the etched figurative historical themes in the library of Eberswalde Technical School, outside Berlin in Germany. Some minimalist offices, such as Caruso St. John or Tony Fretton Architects, have evolved a pared-down approach while using economical materials, and have been influenced as much by minimalism as by Arte Povera, an Italian modern art movement drawing on everyday, sometimes overlooked materials and elements. Yet another practice that can be called minimalist, Tadao Ando Architects, has built its reputation on its exquisite spatial configurations using primarily *in situ* concrete, poured and finished to the highest possible standard. Toyo Ito, a Japanese firm, has incorporated a sophisticated use of artificial light into minimalism. If you want to work in a minimalist office, you will have to show really good detailing in your portfolio, and a sensitivity to and good understanding of the properties of materials. Minimalist offices also very tightly control of the production of design and construction drawings. Whilst all offices do this, in a minimalist office one small error can turn a design from a minimalist one to a mess. You should therefore be ready to work within a pre-established set of rules, and also be willing to work until the detail is right. Whilst minimalist work looks very simple, it takes a lot of time and understanding to do well. If you are a perfectionist, like and can show simple yet compelling spatial and material articulation in your portfolio, this may be destination for you.

### Some Minimalist Architectural Practices

- Caruso St. John, London, UK: www.carusostjohn.com
- Tony Fretton Architects, London, UK: www.tonyfretton.co.uk
- John Pawson London, UK: www.johnpawson.co.uk
- Herzog de Meuron, Basel, Switzerland: http://209.15.129.143/ mono2001/DeMeuronmon_Part2.pdf
- Tadao Ando, Japan: www.andotadao.org
- Toyo Ito, Japan: www.c-channel.com/c00088/index_en.html

### *The New Urbanist Practice*

New Urbanism is mainly a US phenomenon and a response to the growing suburbanization of US cities, with associated sprawl, congestion and absorption of farmland and forest. New Urbanists believe that urban design needs to return to the idea of the traditional nineteenth century European urban block, where residential, commercial and even manufacturing functions are combined, in close proximity to one another. New Urbanists argue that such policies would reduce commuting time, improve the health of city dwellers (by encouraging walking to and from work, shops, school and so on), increase the ratio of green space to urban space by making urban space denser, and foster more interaction between people on the street. New Urbanists have drawn on the ideas of European architects like Rob Krier and Maurice Culot, which in Europe are perhaps most easily visible in the IBA (International Bauausstellung) housing projects built in Berlin before the fall of the Iron Curtain. Whereas in Europe New Urbanism comes in a wide range of architectural styles, in the USA it has become associated with Georgian, Colonial, or Victorian architecture, partly as a way to visually represent the return to the traditional urban block.

The leading New Urbanist practice in the USA is Duany Plater Zyberk, who pioneered New Urbanism in North America, and have been tireless advocates to mayors and urban administrations across the country. Partly due to the growing success of this movement, and partly as a cultural criticism of its stylistic focus, new practices are emerging that embrace New Urbanism's urban strategies, but reject its stylistic preferences as too biased towards a white Anglo-Saxon conception of architectural style in a country where non-whites and non-European immigrants will soon outnumber the white population. If you want to work for a New Urbanist practice, you should have a strong interest in urban planning and design, understand the history of cities, and be able to demonstrate those interests through your design work and research.

Resources

- Congress for the New Urbanism: www.cnu.org
- Duany Plater Zyberk web site readings page: www.dpz.com/literature.htm

Firms

- Allison Ramsey Architects, Beaufort, South Carolina, USA: www.allisonramseyarchitect.com
- Duany Plater Zyberk & Company, Miami/Washington/Charlotte, USA: www.dpz.com
- Porphyrios Associates, London, UK: www.porphyrios.co.uk

## The Postmodernist Practice

Architectural postmodernism emerged as a response to architectural modernism, and particularly criticized modernism for its emphasis on simplicity and standardization, and its rejection of history and popular culture as components of architectural design. The canonical text that introduced postmodernist ideas into architectural culture was *Complexity and Contradiction in Architecture*, by Robert Venturi. Postmodernist architecture is typified by its formal complexity, use of materials for iconic or ironic purposes, figurative elements and historical quotation. Venturi Scott Brown are probably the most well-known firm representing this type of work, although many others sprung up following the publication of the book and the construction of their first projects. Their extension to the National Gallery in London shows just how much they were willing to use historical quotations, and then distort the sources they used, in a highly mannered game of façade rhythms. The work of other postmodern architects is more unusual – the buildings of John Outram for example, fit into this category, but are also relatively free of irony. Rather than drawing on history, Outram draws upon mythology, some of it invented by himself, to create an architecture that carries symbolic narratives. It could also be said that New Urbanism, in its use of historical styles, and the work of historicist architects are both a part of the emergence of architectural postmodernism and it rejection of functionalist design. If you enjoy eclecticism, popular iconography, and the ironic or mythic use or architectural elements, and your work shows complex and contradictory combinations of architectural elements, this could be the destination for you. However, you should not assume postmodern design is easy – you will find that its leading proponents have a deep and broad understanding of architectural history and popular culture, and thus the ironies, juxtapositions and quotations are often much more sophisticated than they might appear to the untrained eye.

Some Postmodernist Practices

• Venturi Scott Brown, Philadelphia, USA: www.vsba.com
• Michael Graves Studio, Princeton/New York, USA: www.michaelgraves.com
• Ricardo Bofill, Barcelona, Spain: www.bofill.com
• John Outram, London, UK: www.johnoutram.com

### Sustainable or Ecological Practice

The emergence of the industrial revolution, and the rise of mass production and mass consumption not only brought advances in information technologies and digital media, but also has faced architects and humanity in general with shrinking energy, spatial and material resources. Sustainable architecture therefore grew out of and is closely linked to various ecological and "green" movements, and deals with the use of ecologically sustainable and energy-efficient use of materials, methods of construction, programming, and maintenance. Green Architecture can include the use of recycled materials and energy conservation to lead to designs with little or no dependence on non-renewable energy sources. In some parts of the world, like Germany or Scandinavia, you will find a high level of interest in these issues, backed by national legislation. Sauerbruch Hutton Architects is a German firm with a strong track record in sustainable design and Passe Kälber Architekten have developed interesting models of shaping air flow through complex spatial configurations (see Chapter 10, Other International Case Studies, for more information). Ken Yeang Associates in Singapore is another firm that integrates principles of sustainability into architectural projects. In the USA, Murphy Jahn have a strong interest in this area.

If you are interested in this subject you should talk to your supervisors or professors, and identify firms and individuals that can provide resources for this body of knowledge as well as contacts to individual firms, and professional journals where positions may be advertised. The US Green Building Council (USGBC) is an organization that promotes building design and construction that are environmentally responsible, healthy, and yet profitable. It also sets standards and guidelines for evaluating environmental performance from a "whole building" perspective over a building's life cycle, providing definitive standards for what constitutes a "green building". The USGBC is a coalition of leaders from across the building industry working to develop the Leadership on Energy and Environmental Design (LEED™) Green Building Rating System™. LEED™ is a voluntary, market-driven building rating system, based on accepted energy and environmental principles, establishing a balance between construction practices and emerging concepts in sustainable and environmentally responsible design. The USGBC has also developed a programme for registering and rating projects that meet the sustainable performance standards, as well-accrediting practitioners with knowledge of green building practices and principles. In order to learn more about green standards, you should identify the individuals who are LEED™ Accredited Professionals™, find firms that focus on this, and once you have obtained a position there ask your supervisors to be assigned to projects that earned LEED™ certification.

Resources

Hagan, S., *Taking Shape: A New Contract Between Architecture and Nature* (Oxford: Architectural Press, 2001)

Some Firms Specializing in Environmental Design and Sustainability

- Sauerbruch Hutton, Berlin, Germany: www.sauerbruchhutton.de
- Passe Kälber, Berlin, Germany: www.passe-kaelber-architekten.com/

- Murphy Jahn, Chicago, USA: www.murphyjahn.com
- Ken Yeang (T.R. Hamzah and Yeang), Malaysia: www.trhamzahyeang.com

Professional Organizations

- US Green Buildings Council: www.usgbc.org
- Centre for Alternative Technology, Machynlleth, Wales, UK: www.eaue.de/winuwd/188.htm

# 3 Other Types of Office

You do not need to gain all of your professional experience in an architectural office. Periods of time spent in related disciplines in the built environment may count towards your required professional experience if they conform to certain criteria. Experience outside an architectural office can also be useful for another reason. It can give you an insight into the skills and practices that consultants contribute to the building process. It can also teach you about the way architects perceive related professionals, and vice versa, giving you a depth of understanding of the pluses and minuses of collaboration for your later career. Some students also get experience in related disciplines because it may be the only employment opportunity close to home, and home may be necessary as a base for a while to pay off a part of student loans. Whichever your situation, considering work in related disciplines may increase the choices available to you later on. Below are some, but certainly not all of the options open to you, and if you think of a discipline that you think may be related to architecture, do get in touch with your mentor and with your professional architectural organizations to check, just in case that experience may be included in internship or professional credit.

## Contractors, Construction, and Project Management

Many year-out students or interns spend some time working in a construction or construction management company. Male students tend to do this more than female students, as the construction industry is still a male-dominated field. Working for a contractor or construction management company may not seem very glamorous, but you can learn an enormous amount about the process of producing a building. Contracting firms differ from construction management and project management firms in that contractors most often coordinate only the production of a building, and provide some of the labour themselves.

Construction management firms on the other hand coordinate the labour of other contractors, and can have a much broader understanding of construction methods than an average-, small-, or medium-sized contractor. A project management firm may coordinate the entire process of designing and producing a building, including organizing the contributions of a diverse array of professional consultants, from the very beginning of the feasibility study stage where the viability of a building is established, to its furnishings and even maintenance once the building is complete. The range of construction or project management by a management firm depends on the nature of the commission, but the interesting part of working for firms of this kind consists of learning different ways to combine and manage consultant and contractor expertise to produce a building.

Working for a contractor will most likely give you more site and construction experience. You may find that you visit sites every day, or become involved in ordering materials, and learn about the cost of different construction systems, or understand how to separate the material and labour components of the cost of a project. In larger construction firms you may well be doing design, as more and more contractors offer a full service to the clients. You may even be working under a licensed architect. In a small contractor's firm you may get to build something on site, though this may depend on whether you already have some construction experience. Having a direct understanding of and learning respect for the work of a contractor, a construction or project manager can be very useful later on in your architectural career. However, working for a construction or construction management firm may mean that tradition, efficiency, and the budget can sometimes become and remain most important, although with the best firms that should not be the case. Design quality may also not be defined in the same way that you encountered in architecture school. If you know that you enjoy the challenges of site organization, construction systems, and cost management, it can be very rewarding to work on "the production side" – if that is the case, try to find a firm with a licensed architect who can be your supervisor so that you can gather as much experience to count for your year-out or internship portfolio. You may even find that you get to do some designing, as sometimes you may well be the most, or the only visually and formally skilled person in the firm.

Resource

Green, R., *Architect's Guide to Running a Job* (Oxford: Architectural Press, 200)

A Few Professional Associations

- Associated Builders and Contractors, USA: www.abc.org
- American Institute of Constructors: www.aicnet.org
- Chartered Institute of Building, UK: www.ciob.org.uk
- Construction Management Association of America: www. cmaanet.org
- Royal Institute of Chartered Surveyors: www.rics.org

A Few Major Construction and Construction Management Firms

- Bovis Lend Lease, UK and International: www.bovis.com
- McHugh Construction, Chicago, USA: www.mchughconstruction.com
- Turner Construction Company, USA: www.turnerconstruction.com

**Engineering**

Engineering firms are usually very closely associated with architectural firms. Sometimes these two areas are covered within a single company; sometimes they offer consulting services to each other. Engineering professionals might supervise some of your training areas and if you decide to work in an engineering firm, but still want to pursue architectural licensing, make sure that you understand how many hours will be accepted. Various engineering disciplines include: civil, environmental, geotechnical, materials testing, mechanical/electrical/plumbing (often referred to as MEP), structural engineering, etc. Some firms made their reputation on the integration of architectural design and engineering (structural engineering in particular), while others are known for their experimentation with new materials and technologies, offering interesting opportunities for integration of sustainable design with material practices. *Progressive Engineer* is an online magazine and resource for information on all disciplines of engineering in the USA. It also has a job board and directories of engineering firms, engineering organizations, and engineering schools. As with many other online services, you can subscribe to the *Progressive Engineer* mailing list and receive regular notifications about various aspects of this field. Different engineering fields have their own professional organizations, which similarly to architectural organizations, offer a wide array of information and resources for the practical experience.

Some Engineering Publications

• Progressive Engineer: www.progressiveengineer.com

Some Professional Associations

• American Society of Civil Engineers: www.asce.org
• Institute of Structural Engineers, UK: www.istructe.org.uk
• Structural Engineering Institute, USA: www.seinstitute.org

Some Engineering Firms

• Arup, UK: www.arup.com
• Dewhurst Macfarlane, London, UK and New York, USA: www.dewmac.com
• Thornton Tomasetti, USA: www.thettgroup.com

**Interior Design**

Some firms specialize in interior design only, but you will also find a number of companies that cover both architectural and interior design. Although interior designers often go through a separate educational and professional training, as an architectural student you should have been expected to develop an understanding of interior design processes and therefore you may be attractive to an interior design firm. Many traditional architectural firms will also rely on smaller interior design and renovation projects since they are less expensive than new construction and often pay higher professional fees. Similar to architectural projects, interior design spans a variety of building types and scales. Some projects might include a single room or a space, while larger buildings might have a series of interior design projects and/or renovations. Interior design involves research and work with vendors.

There are many interior design firms operating independently of architecture firms. They vary in size, and although the largest architectural firm in the world, Gensler, begun by offering interior design services, generally interior design firms are small; many are one-person operations. One-person firms are especially typical for residential design. Many architecture firms also have interior design departments. During economic crises architecture firms often lay off many of their interior designers and reduce the size of the interior design departments. There is a battle for territory raging between architects and interior designers. Interior designers fight for accreditation and licensing in order to exclude the architects from interiors commissions and architects argue that interior designers are not licensed to design buildings, and should therefore not be licensed. Interior designers tend to be narrowly specialized by space type and often consider each space type as a separate professional field. The largest area is in commercial interior design. Next in line is institutional interior design. Residential design is about 4–8% of the industry. Interior designers emphasize more specification writing and, in the USA, code compliance. Specification writing/product specifying can be a painstaking and sometimes a tedious process; however, senior designers need to know it and for an architecture intern this can be a very useful learning experience. Interior design thinking, unlike architectural design, can often be very intuitive. In the USA interior design education evolved from the sphere of home economics, but at the same time often has more courses on art, drawing, and rendering than many architecture schools. In the UK interior design education varies, with the best programmes providing knowledge that includes structural and spatial planning alongside drawing, colour theory, specification writing, and so on.

In an interior design office you will be expected to develop communication skills that enable you to talk to various sales representatives and obtain furniture samples, floor covering samples, colour palettes, etc. Interior design also works on a smaller scale than the scale of a building and you will be engaged in a closer exploration of furniture, materials, surfaces, colour, details, and finishes, including details about lighting, power, and data. You may get to design interesting details and sometimes (depending on the interests and budget of the client) work with highly skilled craftsmen. Interior projects are developed through plan, section and elevation drawings, and through a number of detail drawings. They might also include sketches and three-dimensional renderings that visualize the space in all its materials, textures, and colour. You may be able to work on some construction drawings, though you may not ever work with a structural engineer, and may be heavily involved with specification writing – the careful description of the type and quality of materials used. If you work in a firm that provides interior planning services, you may also become involved in the programming of interior spaces.

### Resources

Pile, J., *Interior Design* (New York: H.M. Abrams, 1995)
A list of the largest interior design firms is available at:
www.interiordesign.net

Some Professional Associations

- American Society of Interior Designers: www.asid.org
- Chartered Society of Designers, UK: www.csd.org.uk
- Interior Decorators and Designers Association, UK: www.idda.co.uk

Some Interior Design Firms

- Gensler, USA and International: www.gensler.com
- Hopping Kovach Grinnell Design Consultants, Canada: www.hkgdesign.com
- Wimberly Allison Tong & Goo (hospitality design): www.watg.com
- Pavlik Design Team (retail): www.pavlikdesign.com
- Gwathmey Siegel & Associates Architects LLC (residential): www.gwathmey-siegel.com

**Landscape Architecture**

Internship and professional experience can also include landscape planning and design. Sometimes these areas are covered within a large architectural firm that also employs landscape architects, but sometimes these services can be provided by an outside consulting landscape architecture firm. It is important to understand that every building is built within a very specific environmental and geophysical context and that this site specificity influences the building design from the very beginning. This context includes the environment, both natural and cultural, planning codes, and regulations, etc. If you work for a landscape architect you may become involved in design, construction drawings, and planting plans. You may also become involved in environmental evaluation, which is conducted through a site study that involves conditions of orientation, climate, topography, and vegetation. It is often conducted in teams of architects and landscape architects, which can sometimes include geotechnical engineers and other consultants with expertise in environmental studies and infrastructural planning. Working in a team evaluating a planning context, you may find yourself studying many regulatory restrictions defined in codes related to parking, zoning, fire, building, environmental hazards, access to utilities, people with disabilities, etc. You will learn the interdependence of many of these systems, and the powerful impact they can have on design.

Resources

Tenant, R., *Professional Practice for Landscape Architects* (Oxford: Architectural Press, 2002)

Some Professional Associations

- The Landscape Institute, UK: www.l-i.org.uk
- American Society of Landscape Architects: www.asla.org
- Australian Institute of Landscape Architects: www.aila.org.au
- Canadian Society of Landscape Architects: www.csla.ca

Some Landscape Architecture Firms

- Dirt Studio, USA: www.dirtstudio.com
- Hargreaves Associates, USA: www.hargreaves.com

## Urban Design and/or Planning

The field of urban design involves the articulation of urban spaces between buildings and, in the USA, the research and creation of urban spatial policy. It often deals with the design of and legislation for public spaces in cities or rural communities, articulating the spatial aspirations of communities and special interest groups. This field straddles architecture, landscape architecture, community activism and planning, and might also involve community participation through presentations, discussions, and workshops. It also overlaps with physical planning, a branch of the discipline that in addition to policy making and analysis deals with strategic planning of the economic and social development of urban and rural spaces and their physical articulation. Urban designers often provide a framework for the work of architects, defining street fronts, block sizes and shapes, circulation patterns and integration of vegetation with the built environment. A lot of urban design projects involve urban and rural renovations at various scales, and improvements of public spaces through re-design of existing transportation patterns, landscaping and building access systems. Although normally bigger in scale, urban design can often also include the detailed design of streetscapes and benches, banners, pavements, and vegetation. Many large cities in particular have recently undergone a renewed interest in central districts and their public spaces, and have introduced improvement initiatives through urban design. Such projects also often include designs for a more accessible and user-friendly environment around riverfronts, lakefronts, and other areas in which a city interacts with the natural environment.

The field of urban design differs enormously between the USA and UK, and Europe. In the USA urban design centres more on the production of urban policy on transportation, employment, taxation, and so forth, with little or no visual exploration of the consequences of urban policies. In the UK and in Europe, however, urban design has a strong visual component and a strong design emphasis. Since urban design revolves around context and culture, you will find many other regional differences in this field, which might lead you to an interesting opportunity to practice internationally. It is therefore also very important that you find out precisely how an urban design firm in a particular country defines its practice, and how your skills might fit its expertise.

Resources

Arida, A., *Quantum City* (Oxford: Architectural Press, 2002)
Barnett, J., *An Introduction to Urban Design* (New York: Harpers Collins, 1982)
Moughtin, J.C., *Urban Design: Method and Technique* (Oxford: Architectural Press, 2003)

Professional Associations

- American Planning Association: www.planning.org
- The Royal Town Planning Institute, UK: www.rtpi.org.uk
- Commonwealth Association of Planners: www.commonwealth-planners.org
- European Council of Town Planners: www.ceu-ectp.org

Some Firms Specializing in Planning

- David Lock Associates, UK: www.davidlock.com
- Clarion Associates, USA: www.clarionassociates.com

**Surveying, Property Management, and Real Estate**

Surveying is an area of practice in the built environment that is important in the UK but does not exist in many other countries. It is unknown in the USA, although in Italy the profession of the "geometra" is fairly close to that of a traditional UK surveyor. It includes the knowledge base needed for the surveying of property, including the estimation of its value, the management of cost estimating for construction, the evaluation and development of construction methods from a cost management perspective, and sometimes the coordination of construction projects, particularly where cost is a paramount issue. Surveying therefore spans an understanding of urban development and property or real estate value, an understanding of construction methods and materials, increasingly the cost of construction management processes, and the production of specifications.

The surveyor in the UK forms an important part in the building production process because she/he is often responsible for the cost control element of the project. The surveyor in the UK is also often responsible for the production of the specification. Whereas in Germany an architect may well take on, during the production of construction drawings, the production of a specification that includes the work of estimating the amounts and costs of materials in a project, in the UK the surveyor, as an independent consultant, often performs that role. The surveyor in the UK will also often act as a middleman or mediator between the client, the architect and the contractor in the area of cost control. Larger surveying firms can often include licensed architects; if they do not, you may still see the idea of gaining expertise at the financial end of the building production process important enough to identify areas of experience that will fit your internship or year-out experience requirements. There are also internal specializations within surveying. For example, surveyors can specialize in particular parts of the building process, such as party wall or rights of light legislation.

Surveying firms are changing enormously, offering services that include and go beyond architecture to embrace property management, and property or real estate development consultancy. The traditional surveyor is becoming a global practitioner, with expertise in building, construction, land, commercial, and residential brokerage; property, project, and facilities management; appraisals and real estate consulting; planning and development; and dispute resolution. Surveyors can also offer strategic advice in the economics, valuation, finance, investment, and management of physical assets that include but are certainly not limited to buildings. Davis Langdon Everest, part of Davis Langdon and Seah International, is a global firm (see Chapter 8, UK Case Studies) that began as a surveying practice but today provides a broad range of services.

Resources

Sirota, D., Introduction, *Essentials of Real Estate Investment* (Chicago: Real Estate Education Company, 1978)
Groak, S., *The Idea of Building* (London: E&F.N.Spon, 1992, pp. 121–129, 142–148, 172–176)
Royal Institute of Chartered Surveyors: www.rics.org

Surveying Practices

• Davis Langdon and Seah International: www.davislangdon.com
• Anstey Horne and Co (party wall and rights of light): web site under construction at time of print

## What Next?

As you can see, applying for a job in an architectural office implies an extensive level of research about professional markets, types of offices, and different specializations within offices. Think carefully about what kind of work you would like to do, where would you like to do it, and then define what is the most appropriate strategy to achieve that goal. Bounce your ideas off friends and your mentor, get involved in your local architectural organization and ask a lot of questions. The more questions you ask, the more you will learn about the profession and the better a choice you will be able to make. This in turn will make you less frustrated with the limitations to your professional experience that you might otherwise not understand. If, however, you find that conventional architectural practice leaves you with a sense of limited horizons, you should look deeper and further still, at critical and emerging architectural practices, the subject of the next chapter.

# 4  Critical and Emerging Practices

In this chapter we will introduce the concept of critical and emerging practices and how these provide alternatives to the types of practical experience outlined in the previous chapter. Working in critical and emerging practices requires some serious thought and planning, as they may not at first appear to fit the requirements of the year out/ internship year. Drawing on various theoretical writings, this chapter explains why critical and emerging practices exist, how they relate to conventional professional practice, why they are important and where you might find such opportunities.[1] We have included theoretical material because critical practice is understood differently in different contexts and theory helps to understand the reasons for the definitions used in this book.

## What is Critical Practice?

Any practice, including architectural practice, has conventions. These conventions become formalized into a system when that practice becomes professionalized. Professions depend on formal conventions because they are by definition organizations whose main purpose is to admit and certify only certain qualified individuals as members.

---

[1]The chapter draws on the writings of the critical theorist Adorno T. and sociologists of professionalism, including Burrage, M., Dingwall, R., Geison, G., Lewis, P., Sarfatti, Larson M. and Torstendahl, R., to explain the formation and reproduction of professions and their values.

To do this they need rules – defining the admission and certification process – that allow aspiring individuals to prepare for, understand and hopefully fit within the profession. These conventions or rules are not neutral. To understand why this is so, it is important to understand some history and theory of professionalism.

The modern professions – including architecture, engineering, and accountancy – formally emerged in the nineteenth century as occupational groups that had to uphold and increase their existing informal social and economic status. New occupations springing from the industrial division of labour, like existing occupations, also tried to professionalize their work and so challenged the authority of traditional professions.

Established and new professions struggled for control of their segment of the marketplace to make sure they had enough well-paid work. Control of the marketplace was and continues to be embodied in the idea of monopoly, which consists of restricted access to certain work practices through certification of only certain individuals. Burrage and Torstendahl explain this aspect of the professions:

> occupations attempt to control market conditions through market
> closure ... Those which are especially successful are the ones which
> we have come to call "the professions".[2]

Monopoly relies on scarcity that in turn raises the market value of the occupation. However, protection of monopoly cannot be achieved by the profession alone. A profession necessarily serves broader interests, usually the interests of socially and economically powerful groups. Such groups are served by professions and in turn help to protect professions' monopoly of practice. This protective partnership influences the conventions and values of a profession, and professions in general do not therefore have full control of either their knowledge or their position within the social order. Instead they depend on the support of more powerful social groups like the state (or the monarchy in earlier times) who have the authority to control licensing and certification laws. In the UK, the Royal Institute of British Architects (RIBA) was created by royal charter in the nineteenth century to protect professional architectural interests, and in the twentieth century the Architects' Registration Council of the UK (ARCUK), which then became Architects' Registration Board (ARB), was created through government legislation to make sure all architects were subject to licensing law. In the USA, individual states

---

[2]Burrage, M. and Torstendahl, R., *Professions in Theory and History: Rethinking the Study of the Professions* (London: Sage Publications,1990); p. 25.

have passed legislation protecting the title and practice of architecture and have routes through which certification in one state makes it easier to be certified in another.

During the era of the nation state, many professions in the USA, Britain and in Europe sought and received state endorsement through state legislation defining and protecting the professional's title (only a licensed professional can call him/herself an architect) and, in many cases, protection of practice itself (only a licensed professional can design buildings over a certain size). At the same time, professional conventions were also influenced by the interests of the profession itself – a kind of internal regulation, albeit always within a broader set of social constraints.

To be given the right to monopoly, the professional has had to fulfil an unspoken social contract with the state. Sociologists studying the professions offer an interesting explanation for this. The state (and previously the monarchy) gives special privileges to professionals in a state/ profession alliance because professional knowledge, by lying close to potential sources of social conflict, both represents and threatens state interests:

> The professions are licensed to carry out some of the most danger-
> ous tasks of our society – to intervene in our bodies, to intercede for
> our prospects of future salvation, to regulate the conflict of rights and
> obligations between social interests. Yet in order to do this, they must
> acquire guilty knowledge (the priest is an expert on sin, the doctor on
> disease, the lawyer on crime) and the ability to look at these matters
> in comparative and, hence, relative terms. This is the mystery of the
> professions. Their privileged status is an inducement to maintain their
> loyalty in concealing the darker sides of their society and in refraining
> from exploiting their knowledge for evil purposes.[3]

Dingwall and Lewis believe that this function, the professions' resolution of potential social conflict and protection of dangerous knowledge, explains their historical closeness to political power. It also explains the continued willingness of political interests to uphold professional interests.

Architecture is no exception. Architecture symbolically represents the laws of property on which economic and social order rests. It also acts as one of the most public means of regulating social conflict through symbolic representation and the ordering of spatial patterns of behaviour. Architecture that is critical of social norms is relatively rare, rarer for example than critical literature or dystopian film. Architecture comparable

---

[3]Dingwall, R. and Lewis, P. (eds), *The Sociology of the Professions: Lawyers, Doctors and Others* (London: The Macmillan Press Ltd., 1983); p. 5.

to Dadaism, Situationism, agit-prop, gothic horror and dystopian science fiction is difficult to practice because this would turn into reality the negative and dangerous social aspects of professional knowledge on whose exclusion the nature of professionalism relies. However, architectural practices that are critical of prevailing professional architectural conventions, although still difficult to practice, are possible. Such practices are possible because they only question the professional boundaries regulated by architects rather than those regulated by broader social interests.

If the professions depend on monopoly, and if the state and the public need the guarantee that professionals will not abuse their knowledge, the production process of the professional has to ensure that both sides of the professional social contract (scarcity and exclusivity of professionals through monopoly, and safety of the public through legislation, practical conventions and certification) are successfully maintained. Control of part of that process lies within the professions and their practices, and partial change to that process can occur through critical practice and, just as importantly, through education.

Educational change is just as important as change in practice because most professionals do not sell tangible goods but sell their knowledge in the form of services. This turns their knowledge into a commodity. However, in order to maintain scarcity and exclusivity, that knowledge cannot be freely reproducible, as it could be through text, for example. Instead, the sociologist Magali Sarfatti Larson argues that it must become "inseparable from the person of the expert ... [and] thus be gradually constructed into a special kind of property".[4] Professional knowledge has to become embodied in the very being of the professional. She explains how this takes place:

> professional work, like any other form of labour, is only a *fictitious* commodity; it cannot be detached from the rest of life, be stored or mobilised ... it follows therefore that the *producers themselves have to be produced* if their products or commodities are to be given a distinctive form.[5]

The profession, and especially its education process, therefore becomes the setting through which the values of the profession and of the professionals themselves is produced and reproduced. For the architectural

---

[4]Sarfatti Larson, M. In: Haskell, T.L. (ed.), *The Authority of Experts* (Bloomington: Indiana University Press, 1984); p. 34; parentheses by Rüedi Ray, K.
[5]*Ibid.* p. 14; Larson's italics.

profession this education process includes, of course, the year out or internship year.

External state and internal professional interests are not always fully compatible, and sometimes the state can be more flexible than the professions. Within education during the era of state licensing, the profession/ state alliance has led to mutual compromise as professions tried to limit entry of the same social classes empowered by twentieth century state liberal democratic expansion of education. The state has had only limited impact – in contrast to non-professional education, standards of admission, and certification in professional education have generally remained higher, attrition rates greater, and the education process longer than other, non-professional occupations.

The characteristic features of a profession, which usually leads to a longer education process with a professional training/internship component, include:

1. formal technical training (formal design, technical, and professional education);
2. intellectual skills (formal historical and theoretical education);
3. an institutionalized setting that certifies quality and competence (such as both the university and the professional certifying organization);
4. demonstrable skills in the pragmatic application of this formal training (this is what the year out or internship year is for);
5. institutional mechanisms ensuring that knowledge will be used in a socially responsible role (professional code of ethics).[6]

The categories of formal technical training, demonstrable pragmatic skills, intellectual ability and social responsibility fulfil the social contract that professional knowledge be both useful and safe. It thus appears no longer to be dangerous knowledge. Standardized examinations and certification maintain the homogeneity and scarcity of professional knowledge. Together they provide a minimum standard by which the newly qualified professional gains the state protection (of title) necessary to secure monopolistic practices.

The architectural profession has effected these features, with greater or lesser degrees of success, by incorporating them into education and certification processes. The first four desired characteristics of the professional define major areas of the architectural curriculum such as constructional knowledge, history and theory of architecture, professional

---

[6]Geison, G. (ed.), *Professions and Professional Ideologies in America* (Chapel Hill: University of North Carolina Press, 1983); p. 4; summary and adaptation to architecture by Rüedi Ray, K.

studies, and practical experience (the year out or internship year). However, because most of this knowledge is reproducible, these features do not alone create and maintain professional monopoly. Reproducibility through education and publication makes these professional attributes available to competing occupational groups, who have, of course, made use of them. If these were the only types of professional architectural knowledge, the monopoly of the architect could not be maintained.

The year out or internship year structure, which allows only certain kinds of experience, and privileges work under a licensed architect, helps to ensure both scarcity (not all students find this ideal work setting) and safety (the transmission of professional knowledge from the supervisor to the trainee occurs under the supervision of an existing member of the profession).

However, the value of the professions also rests on the elevation of certain traits to a "natural" status beyond conscious learning. This has, until recently, raised the market value of professionals above that of their competitors. Larson affirms that professional competence is indeed attained unconsciously and consciously:

> effects [of professional education] are measured in the non-physical constraint of accepted definitions, or internalised moral and epistemological norms. It is in one sense impersonal, for it makes the most general knowledge claims; yet it is also deeply personal, in that the individual who internalises the general and special discourses of his or her own culture experiences them as natural expressions or extensions of his or her own will and reason.[7]

The terms "natural" and "will" are important because they place areas of professional expertise beyond conscious cultural criticism. The illusion of individual and professional freedom comes from the "naturalization" of socially created professional knowledge into personal will. For example, when architectural educators speak of a "born designer", they are in fact describing someone who has learned, consciously or otherwise, to fit the conventions of a professional, rather than someone who was actually (and impossibly) born with the ability to design.

In addition to serving the interests of and deriving benefit from the state, the conventions and values of the professions also serve the interests of business, because business now forms the most powerful interest in the world. Many of the professions have become more business-like as

---

[7]Sarfatti Larson, M. *op.cit.* pp. 35–36.

first world political economies have shifted from the industrialism of the nation-state to multinational capitalism, and the professions' patronage has shifted from institutional public to corporate private clients. This too has created some compromises as free-market principles have necessarily eroded professional monopoly, and business ethos has placed professional ethics under greater pressure.

Critical practices have emerged as a challenge to both the explicit and implicit conventions of practice, and the interests of powerful social groups. In the case of professions, critical practice has also, more successfully, questioned both the stated and unstated values of the profession itself. This questioning of values and practices has ranged from critiques of unconscious assumptions about the identity of the professional, to the position of professional practice in relation to dominant economic, social, and cultural interests, as well as to the boundaries conferring legitimacy on some practices and not on the others.

Indeed, the idea of critical practice is integral to the idea of democracy. In his book, *Critical Models: Interventions and Catchwords*, Theodor Adorno proposes that critique is an essential part of any democratic societal, educational, professional, and institutional model. Adorno argues that critique and its practical counterpart, critical practice, are both signs of political, personal, and professional maturity and integrity. Critical practice shows that one can think and act independently, and therefore can resist and even change established and uncritically received values:

> Critique is essential to all democracy. Not only does democracy require the freedom to criticize and need critical impulses. Democracy is nothing less than defined by critique. This can be recalled simply in the historical fact that the conception of the separation of powers, upon which every democracy is based, from Locke to Montesquieu and the American constitution up to today, has its lifeblood in critique.[8]

Adorno defines critical practice as resistance through thinking and doing that can decompress rage inflicted upon oneself and upon others through oppression and exploitation. He sees critical practice exposing, denying and changing established and uncritically received values. He calls for the cultivation of critical personality rather than a narrowly defined, scientifically based, and critically unexamined professional training.

---

[8]Adorno, T.W., *Critical Models: Interventions and Catchwords* (New York: Columbia University Press, 1998); pp. 281–282.

This has interesting implications for the year out or internship year, as we will explain later.

The architectural profession is regarded by some, particularly those who have not traditionally had access, as in need of revision. It has significantly lower percentages of women and minorities than, say, medicine or law.[9] Critics see the democratization of education and a stronger emphasis on community-based, non-elite forms of practice as an important avenue for future practices. Others regard the restriction of legitimate architectural practice to the architectural office as another form of exclusivity. Such critics see real estate development and design-build (traditionally seen as undermining the impartiality of the professional) as critical practices. Yet others see the creation of imaginary spatial environments (whether drawn or digitally animated) as stigmatized for their lack of "reality". Other groups argue that critical environmental practices, because buildings in first world economies consume enormous amounts of non-renewable energy resources, can transform architecture's contributions to the ecological well-being of the planet. Yet others argue that critical writings on architecture constitute critical practice that can help to change the conventions of architectural education and the profession. Such writings confirm that the architectural profession, its education processes, and its publication outlets still often remain conservative and exclusive.[10] The many forms of critical practice have an important role to play in expanding the horizon of the architectural profession so that it can better serve the needs of democratic society and be more inclusive in its membership, knowledge, and practices.

If one agrees that a critical practice exists to expose and transform unconscious values and conventions, then it becomes important to

[9]RIBA 2003 report on why women are leaving the architectural profession; http://www.riba.org/go/RIBA/News/Press_2693.html?q=report%20on%20gender (accessed 15 July 2004); American Institute of Architects (AIA) information on race and gender: http://www.aia.org/diversity/default.asp (accessed 15 July 2004). These web sites confirm that close to 90% of licensed members of both the AIA and the RIBA consist of white men.
[10]Garry Stevens' The Favored Circle (Cambridge, MA: MIT Press, 2002) sets out a powerful critique of both unconscious and conscious class assumptions of the architectural profession. C. Greig Crysler's Writing Spaces (London: Routledge, 2002) shows how intellectual communities in the built environment – including those centered on architectural history, theory, planning, and geography – uphold critically unexamined conventions related to their ideas and practices. Leslie Kanes Weisman's Discrimination by Design (Champaign, IL: University of Illinois Press, 1994), Kathryn Anthony's Designing for Diversity: Gender, Race, and Ethnicity in the Architectural Profession (Champaign, IL: University of Illinois Press, 2001), and Melvin Mitchell's The Crisis of the African American Architect (Lincoln, NE: iUniverse Inc., 2002) examine gender and racial inequalities in the architectural profession.

question certain basic assumptions about conventional practice and instead value practices that take a different approach. The most common assumption about conventional architectural practice is that it is about the design of buildings for construction – that spatial production rather than image production is what architects coordinate and do. Yet architects for the most part do not build. They draw, write, make models, calculate, and talk. Contractors for the most part build, and in many cases do not need architects to do so. The year out or internship year actually involves only a relatively small amount of site experience, and has no requirements for hands-on construction work. The main task of an architect is working with systems of representation, whether with digital imaging, design drawings, construction documentation or specification writing which then require interpretation and construction by another profession to create a building. Yet conventionally, architects who run critical and emerging practices that only produce drawings or animations are called paper architects, and their architecture is called paper architecture. Conventional architectural practice is never seen as paper architecture. Making this contradiction explicit is important, because many critical and emerging practices begin, and a few remain as practices that produce only drawings. Yet despite the social and political power of images in an age of media and communication, and a migration of students from architecture to the film and video game industries, the paper architecture debate appears to have had little impact beyond the profession. It has led to career successes by architects producing and selling drawings within a gallery setting, as well as the relative standing of architecture schools (which cannot conventionally be associated with making buildings) and the majority of practices that begun with "paper projects" have transformed into practices with conventional building commissions.

Critical practices can cover quite a few types of activity, some of which can form part of the Internship Development Program (IDP) or the Professional Experience and Development Record (PEDR). They can focus on social critique (dealing with class, race, ethnic, gender, disability, and age inequalities), on environmental critique (dealing with ecological and environmental solutions), on design critique (dealing with systems of representation and taste), on activism (working as participants and advocates in community empowerment), on teaching (this is acceptable if it forms part of community service), and on construction (ranging from installations in exhibition settings to actual construction of buildings). You will find that in your IDP or PEDR documents certain amounts of time are allocated to such categories of practice. In this book we are suggesting that these conventional categories may have more unconventional, yet still professionally legitimate interpretations that may allow you to look for and work, at least for some time, in practices or situations that do not immediately appear to meet conventional expectations. The crucial element to remember is, of course, that your IDP or PEDR has to be supervised and signed by a licensed or registered architect who needs to agree with these interpretations. This means that if you want to gain the kind of experience outlined in this chapter, you will need to find a critical practice that includes a sympathetic licensed or registered architect. There are numerous architects who engage in this kind of practice, although the definitions these architects use to identify their offices as critical practices do vary, and therefore are the subject on ongoing debate. Some of these practices are included in Chapters 8–10.

Critical practices overlap with, but are not seen as being the same as emerging practices. Emerging practices in architecture are usually entrepreneurial in spirit, less concerned with a critical exposure of and transformation of the profession, and more concerned with seeking new opportunities in emerging cultural, technological, and social markets at the edges of, and often entirely beyond currently accepted professional architectural practice. Emerging practices become critical of professional conventions when their work becomes sufficiently different from core professional practice that it becomes difficult for their practitioners to work within professional architectural conventions. At this point in time work for an emerging practice can slip outside the requirements for the year out, the professional code of conduct, or phases of the architectural work plan.

A key emerging practice is one centring on the use of digital technologies. It can be seen both as an emerging practice (responding to new technologies) and a critical practice (questioning the accepted way of producing building designs and fabrication). However it may be regarded, new information technologies, design disciplines, and the construction industry are coming together in ways once unimaginable, and their union is changing how we use buildings, as well as how they are designed and built. The term digital media encompasses many information technologies, providing not only new design tools, but also redefining architectural representation and modes of construction. Digital media make extensive use of digital technologies to address the relationship between actual and virtual environments, and actively pursue alternative forms of architectural and urban space. Digital media deal with electronically based methods and techniques of design and construction, thus questioning traditional formal, material, and programmatic aspects of architecture. Generally speaking, the use of digital media in architecture has two main modes – animation and digital fabrication, sometimes also called mass customization. Virtual reality utilizes various animation software packages, such as *Maya*, *Softimage*, *3D Studio Max/Viz*, and *Form Z*, in order to speculate about new kinds of space. On the other hand, some of these programmes can also be used to build models through laser cutters and ultimately to translate into fabrication software systems to produce formally complex but mathematically calculable structures. By balancing computer visualization techniques, digital design of three-dimensional spaces, animation, and web-based interactive technologies, digital media strategies are beginning to profoundly transform traditional design processes and allow experimentation with new materials and interactive environments. Some firms specializing in digital media, video, and animation include Diller and Scofidio, Digit-All studio, Garofalo Architects, LynnForm, and Studio Asymptote. Professional organizations that have emerged in this area include Acadia, SIGGRAPH and Inter-Society for the Electronic Art (ISEA) among others.

If working for a critical or emerging practice provides you with the experience you need to successfully complete your practical training, you will be able in turn to mentor others if you wish to set up your own critical or emerging practice in the future. As with critical practice, if you choose to work for emerging practice and want to include a significant part of that experience in your IDP form or PEDR, you will need to be supervised by a licensed architect. You will need to discuss and agree the appropriate categories of experience to fit the normal process of becoming a licensed professional with your supervisor and mentor. That process, and its rules and supervision procedures, can embrace traditional, critical and emerging practices, and forms the subject of the next two chapters.

# 5 The Year Out and Beyond: Becoming an Architect in the UK

In this chapter you will learn about the process of becoming a registered architect in the United Kingdom. We will introduce you to the two legal bodies that are involved in shaping the guidelines for architectural education and professional experience leading up to registration, the Architects' Registration Board (ARB) of the United Kingdom, and the Royal Institute of British Architects (RIBA).

## Governing Bodies

### The Architects' Registration Board

In order to register and practice as an architect in the UK, it is necessary to comply with the requirements of the Architects' Registration Board (ARB). The ARB was formed by an Act of Parliament called the Architects' Act in 1997 and is the independent statutory regulator for all architects registered in the UK. Its task is "to protect the interests of consumers and to safeguard the interests of architects".[1] Without being listed on the ARB's register, you may not practice under the title of architect.

The Architects' Act 1997 gives "the responsibility for prescribing the qualifications and practical training experience required for entry onto the

---

[1] Architects' Registration Board: www.arb.org.uk

UK Register of Architects".[2] The ARB is therefore responsible for the standards an individual must attain in order to become, and continue to practice as an architect. In order to carry out this role, ARB publishes strictly controlled criteria that set out the minimum standards a student must acquire at each of the 3 stages of becoming an architect. These stages are known as Parts 1, 2, and 3. Once registered as an architect, you are bound by the ARB Code of Professional Conduct. The Code of Professional Conduct is taken extremely seriously by ARB and it gives strict guidelines on the conduct of an architect. Any registered architect who fails to maintain the level of professionalism and skill required may be disciplined and ultimately removed from the register by the ARB.

Resource

• ARB web site: www.arb.org.uk

### The Royal Institute of British Architects

The Royal Institute of British Architects (RIBA) is an institute that has "been promoting architecture and architects since being awarded a Royal Charter in 1837".[3] Its mission is to "advance architecture by demonstrating benefit to society and promoting excellence within the profession".[4] Unlike ARB, the RIBA is a member organization with 30,000 members in the UK and worldwide who include student, graduate, and affiliate members. Those members who have completed their professional qualification have the status of Chartered Architect. Unlike the ARB, the RIBA operates as a Professional Institute, providing a range of advisory and information services for its members, to support them in their day-to-day practice of architecture.

The RIBA, like the ARB, upholds a Code of Conduct, which applies to any architect who chooses to join the RIBA. The requirements of the code are pretty much the same as for ARB and failure to comply may again result in disciplinary action by RIBA and/or ARB. Whereas the ARB "prescribes" qualifications through a mainly paper-based scrutiny, the RIBA continues its long established system of course "validation", built around visits to architecture schools and a process of peer review.

---

[2]See *supra* 1.
[3]www.riba.org.uk
[4]See *supra* 3.

Resource

• The RIBA web site: www.riba.org.uk

## The Setting and Monitoring of Professional Education and Qualifications by ARB and RIBA

The gaining of qualifications and practical experience by the architectural student is strictly controlled, both by ARB and RIBA who work together in order to ensure standards are upheld at every level of education and practice both by students of architecture and registered architects. The ARB has responsibility for the legal register of architects and has the statutory responsibility for holding the prescribed list of qualifications in the UK. RIBA membership and course validation is optional for architects and schools of architecture. There are currently 36 schools of architecture in the UK with courses validated by the RIBA and prescribed by the ARB, which means that their professional education content complies with both ARB and RIBA requirements. The validation and prescription process is repeated in every school every 4 years, and schools/courses can and sometimes do lose their professional recognition. It is, therefore, vital that should you intend to study at a school in the UK, particularly if you see this as a way to enter the job market, you ensure that a school is delivering courses that will give you the relevant exemptions to ARB and RIBA requirements necessary on your journey to becoming an architect.

Resource

• A complete list of RIBA validated architecture schools and courses/ programmes: www.architecture.com

## Becoming a Registered Architect in the UK

Under normal circumstances, to register as an architect in the UK, a student would embark on and successfully complete the course of study and practice as outlined below. That means successfully completing:

(i)   a 3-year undergraduate honours degree (B.A. or B.Sc.) in Architecture, gaining exemption from Part 1 of the professional examination;
(ii)  a 12-month period of post-Part 1 Professional Experience and Development Employment, working under a fully qualified registered architect in an architectural practice;

(iii) a 2-year postgraduate diploma in Architecture gaining exemption from the Part 2 examination;

(iv) a minimum 12-month period of post-Part 2 Professional Experience and Development Employment, working under a fully qualified registered architect in an architectural practice, leading to sitting the Part 3 Professional Practice and Management examinations.

The total minimum length of the process of becoming a registered architect in the UK is, under normal circumstances, therefore 7 years. The two minimum 12-month periods of post-Parts 1 and 2 Practical Training are the relevant periods that this book tries to address.[5]

### The Education Process

Each of the three parts of the education of an architect in the UK is designed to instil and examine a student's competence in the range of skills, as well as the breadth and depth of professional development necessary to being a fully independent practising architect.

It is quite usual for students in the UK to study for their individual qualifications at different schools of architecture. Despite this, students in the UK do tend to undertake their post-Part 1, Stage 1 Professional Experience and Development studies whilst registered at the University where they gained their undergraduate degree, particularly as some schools integrate their professional practice teaching within their undergraduate programme. The extent to which this occurs varies enormously and we highly recommend that you research the different options offered by different schools. There is, for example, at least one undergraduate programme in the UK where students complete 1 week of work experience in an architect's practice during their final undergraduate year. This kind of experience can give a student a "head-start" when looking for a year out placement.

Other schools offer a sequence of study and professional experience where Part 1 is gained after 4 years of study, the third being the year out. The choice of school depends considerably on the skills and interests of the particular student, so you should find out the different routes to qualification as an architect that schools offer. You will also find that

---

[5]There are some variations between RIBA and ARB professional experience employment. The RIBA is readier to accept worldwide experience post-Part 1, but has a firmer requirement for post-Part 2 experience to be spent in the UK. Students and graduates should always check their individual plans with both bodies if they think there is a risk they may not be recognized.

there are now a number of specialisms and "pathways", you can choose to follow on your journey to exemption from the Part 1 examination. This advice relates mainly to undergraduate programmes, and as it is likely you will already be enrolled at a school of architecture when you read this book, your options will already have been set. However, you should still find out exactly what the requirements of your school are, as they may affect how you should proceed with the second 12 months of your practical experience. If you have not yet made a selection of your undergraduate programme, looking at the structure for getting professional experience may help you to make a more informed decision.

## Variations

Part-Time Studies

There are also variations to the minimum 7 years of study and practice outlined above. Some students in the UK opt to study part-time. Not all architecture schools offer this as an option, but those that do usually involve an individual studying on a day release system for 5–6 years to gain Part 1. The way you would record your practical experience as a part-time student is different to the process followed by a full-time student. Some courses allow work produced in the office to become a part of the academic learning and evaluation process. Also, some part-time experience can gain you exemption from one or both of the post-Part 1 year out and Part 2 Practical Experience requirements.

## Resources

- For examples of architecture schools offering part-time courses go to www.careersinarchitecture.net. This is part of the RIBA www. architecture.com web site which lists all RIBA validated courses in the UK and worldwide, and includes all prescribed courses in the UK.

## Foreign Qualifications

Any individual who has qualified in another country and wishes to practice as an architect in the UK must undergo a rigorous portfolio inspection and oral examination in order to gain exemption from or a pass in (whichever is appropriate) Parts 1 and 2, and to be allowed to sit Part 3. If you have qualifications obtained in another country outside of the UK or European Union (EU), and want to gain professional experience in the UK that will count towards you becoming a registered architect in the UK, you will be required to demonstrate that you have experienced and achieved a similar standard, complexity, and rigour in your studies and practice as you would have undergone had you-embarked upon a course of architectural study in the UK. It is quite often the case that individuals practising as architects outside of the UK are required to undertake further study and examinations in this country before being eligible to sit their Part 3 examinations and, if successful, to register with the ARB and qualify for full professional ("chartered") membership of the RIBA. For more information see *How a foreign architect can apply to register as a UK architect* towards the end of this chapter.

Resources

• ARB web site: www.arb.org.uk
• RIBA web site: www.riba.org.uk

## The Professional Experience and Development Process

As already stated, in order to sit your Part 3 examinations and become an architect, the ARB and RIBA require that you must have undertaken a minimum of 24 months of Professional Experience and Development Training, which must be completed *after* the start of an architectural course and *before* sitting the Part 3 examination. A minimum of 12 months of this experience ("Stage 2") must be undertaken in the UK *after* passing or gaining exemption from the Part 2 examination. It is usual and recommended that a student architect completes the other 12 months during the post-Part 1 Stage 1, although this is not always the case. Diploma course programmes prefer students to have had a year out before coming back for the final 2 years of study, but if there is an economic downturn many schools will accept students for graduate studies without full practical experience, or will accept other kinds of employment experience. If that is the case, that does not mean that this same experience will count towards your 24 months needed to sit the Part 3 examination, and you will therefore need to get 24 months of practical experience after getting your diploma and getting exemption from the Part 2 examination.

### Year One: Stage 1 Professional Experience

The year out is the name colloquially given to the Stage 1 or professional experience year between undergraduate and advanced diploma course study within the UK system.[6] It may consist of 12 months of continuous employment in an architectural practice, or shorter periods in a range of practices in the UK and elsewhere, and is the first part of an architect's professional training. The year of practical experience gained after you have taken the Part 2 examination is not called the year out. The 12 months or so of your year out are a critical element because this period forms the foundation for subsequent professional experience, and for many students it is the first encounter with professional experience. It is an important and integral part of an architects' education and offers you the opportunity to apply, usually for the first time, what you have learnt during your undergraduate studies, and apply it to the roles and responsibilities of an architect procuring buildings within the UK building industry. The year out also offers a first exposure to the processes of the management of an architectural practice.

***Year Two: Stage 2 Professional Experience***

The second year of your 24-month professional experience period will contain more advanced experience of the work of an architect. You may well be asked to assist a partner in the production of design and construction drawings, and will be beginning to prepare for your Part 3 examination. Depending on the geographical location of your employment, you may be attending evening classes in professional practice to prepare you for the examination, or will be planning to take a short, full-time course instead. Whichever the case, you should be reading extensively about the detailed aspects of each of the work stages of a project, and testing that knowledge on the project or projects you have in hand.

Gaining thorough professional knowledge in this second part of your professional experience is not only very useful for sitting the Part 3 examination, but may be very useful to your office. Often, the student in their second year of professional experience has the most up to date knowledge in the office on the building contract. This may sound strange, but it is likely that the partners in your office only have time to take the minimum amount of hours needed for Continuing Professional Development (CPD), whereas you will probably be spending at least 3 or 4 hours a week on amassing professional knowledge, and, if taking a part-time professional practice course, may have also access to new interpretations of building

---

[6]Postgraduate study in the UK describes the same level of study as graduate study in the USA and Canada.

legislation through the guest speakers in the course. If this is the case, ask the partner in your office to give you feedback on how that new information might apply to your project.

## General Rules: Time

### Minimum Periods of Experience

Your professional experience is recorded in 3-month periods and therefore it is possible to tailor your experience around opportunities that arise – in other words, neither are you obliged to stay with a practice for more than 3 months, nor is the firm obliged to keep you. Obviously, if you have found a great fit, then staying is a good idea. It is important that if you do change positions, and if you want your experience of architectural practice to contribute to your Part 3 examinations, your employment must be under the direct supervision of a registered architect and should mainly or wholly have taken place within the UK. Having said this, the RIBA encourage students to gain some professional working experience beyond UK practice during their Stage 1 Professional Experience.

### Exceptions and Variations

Currently, periods of work of less than 3 months are acceptable only in certain circumstances (except where they are mandatory), and again these would be *in addition* to the requirements outlined previously. Permissible periods of work of less than 3 months include the following:

- A *maximum* period of 3 months working under the direct supervision of a person working in an activity related to architectural practice. This could include architectural journalism, building construction, or exhibition design.
- A *maximum* of 5 working days out of the total 24 months for voluntary or community activity under the direct supervision of a person engaged in that activity.
- A *minimum* of 10 working days attendance or related study leading to RIBA/ARB recognized professional qualification.
- A *minimum* of 35 hours a year of CPD.

### Resource

- For full details visit the RIBA Professional Experience and Development Record web site at www.pedr.co.uk

**General Rules: Supervision**

*Working for an Architect Registered in the UK*

The strictly controlled nature of becoming and practising as an architect in the UK means that you are required by the ARB and RIBA to gain experience working under an architect registered in the UK. Most UK year out students work in medium to large architects' practices. It is unusual, but not unheard of, for a student to work for a developer or other type of practice within the building industry, but if that is an option of interest to you, you would need to do so under the supervision of an architect registered in the UK. That architect may not be the principal or partner of the firm, but needs to be a normal and permanent employee of the firm.

*Your Professional Advisor and Employment Mentor*

In order for employment experience to be a valid part of your post-Parts 1 and 2 Professional Experience and Development required for the Part 3 examination, it must be carried out under the supervision of a tutor who is your *Professional Advisor*. Within the office you must also be directly supervised by a qualified and registered architect, known as your *Employment Mentor*. Your Professional Advisor should advise you about which kinds of work form the appropriate type of professional experience meeting your professional experience requirements, and should act as your advocate with your Employment Mentor (to help you get these). Your Employment Mentor is there to help you get as many of those kinds of experiences possible within the opportunities and constraints of work patterns in your office. For more information on the roles of the Professional Advisor and Employment Mentor please see the following text.

*Exceptions and Variations: Experience Abroad*

Gaining some experience abroad as part of the year out between your undergraduate and postgraduate degrees is encouraged by the RIBA and permitted by the ARB on an individually negotiated basis. It is not currently acceptable to the ARB and RIBA for you to be working outside of the UK for significant periods of time during the post-Part 2 period. The only exception to this rule is if the experience abroad is *in addition* to your total minimum of 24 months. A maximum 12-month period of experience during training in a UK-based firm whose work is wholly or mostly outside of the UK maybe allowed during the post-Part 2 period.

RIBA requirements are less flexible about this and graduates wanting their work experience to count towards Part 3 professional experience requirements are always advised to check non-UK work experience plans with both bodies. It is, however, acceptable for you to gain some experience (e.g. completing a site survey or inspection) abroad, for example if your office has work in other countries. In this instance, the work must again be carried out under the supervision of an architect registered in the UK.

*Supervision by Other Professionals*

These rules are designed to ensure that the majority of your experience is obtained under the supervision of an architect whose work is subject to the construction, management, and legal constraints, practices and knowledge normal to the UK so as to provide a sound preparation for taking the RIBA Examination in Professional Practice and Management (Part 3). In addition to the experience listed so far, you are also allowed a *maximum* of 12 months working under the direct supervision of a qualified chartered professional in the field of building construction in the UK.[7] For most students this experience is likely to be in *addition* to the 24 months of professional experience gained under the supervision of a UK practising registered architect. This particular kind of additional experience can give you a greater understanding of the roles of professionals other than architects within the building industry and can be of particular value should you choose to work as an architect within a multi-disciplinary practice.

*Teaching Experience*

You are also permitted, for a *maximum* of 12 months, to teach on an ARB and RIBA validated course in architecture or engage in architectural research directly related to professional architectural practice in the UK. Again, for most this experience is likely to be in addition to your 24 months of supervised practical training under a UK practising and registered architect. Again, check your individual status by visiting the ARB and RIBA web sites and getting advice.

---

[7]This would generally be during the Stage 1 (year out). Again, the RIBA is more open to the part that the gaining of wider industry experience can play in the 24 months of professional experience requirement. Again you are advised to check the ARB web site and www.pedr.co.uk and get individual advice from both bodies if needed.

## Other Professional Experience

As already mentioned above, many students choose to gain more experience than the minimum 24 months required by ARB and RIBA to give them the advantage they feel may be necessary when competing for work in a post-Part 3 context. However, it is advised that if you choose to do this, you follow the ARB and RIBA rules as outlined above to gain maximum benefit from your extended experience. Remember that this experience must be in addition to the minimum 24 months of supervised professional experience necessary in order to be eligible to take the Part 3 examination. It is therefore essential that you plan your professional experience carefully and gain advice if you have any doubts.[8] Under certain circumstances a mature student with a long record of experience may be exempted from one or both of the 12-month practical experience requirements.

## Employment Status

Employment during your year out must be full-time (i.e. 35 hours per week), although the RIBA will accept employment of at least 20 hours a week for those who need to work shorter hours because of family care responsibility.[9] As employment for a period of less than 3 months continuous service in is not acceptable as a valid part of your professional training experience, short-term, freelance or agency employment and self-employment is neither appropriate nor acceptable when training to become an architect.

# The Professional Experience and Development Record

## What is It and Where to Find It

Before embarking on the year out, you must register online with the RIBA's Professional Experience and Development Scheme and complete an RIBA Professional Experience and Development Record (known as

---

[8]It is important to note that in some circumstances you can have *too much* experience. If you are in a situation where you have already had more than 12 months experience outside of the UK, you will need to get advice. If you are registered on an Undergraduate Architecture Degree or Postgraduate Diploma in Architecture, you can ask your Professional Practice Advisor within your institution. Otherwise, you will need to contact the RIBA's Education department for guidance.
[9]Should this be the case, the student will have to work for a longer period than the minimum of 24 months.

a PEDR). This is a digital record of your experience and training and is signed every 3 months by you, your Employment Mentor and your Professional Advisor. Its purpose is to confirm that you have gained the appropriate experience. The document is an essential element of your Part 3 examination and will often be required by a School of Architecture when you apply for a place on a postgraduate diploma (Part 2) course, as evidence you have completed a year out.

The PEDR is a precise record of the range and diversity of experience gained whilst employed. It is recorded on a quarterly Record Sheet, an example of which can be viewed on the RIBA's web site at www.pedr.co.uk. The Record Sheet is just like a timesheet, and lists all of the key functions an architect would normally fulfil, organized into Work Stages. The PEDR form is designed to indicate your supervised experience to your Professional Advisor and future Part 3 examiner. Through its quarterly signature and feedback from your Professional Advisor and Employment Mentor, it also enables you to evaluate every 3 months the experience you have or have not gained, and try to fill under-served areas with requests for changes or additions to your responsibilities in the office.

**Recording Work Stages and Work Status**

Within the profession the stages of the procurement of a project and the activities in which an architect would engage are always divided up into Work Stages. The Work Stages are listed ranging from A to H, and each stage has subheadings describing the activities that usually occur during that stage. You are required to fill in the number of hours you have engaged in a particular work stage per month, and to state whether you have been a participant in the activity or an observer. You can gain experience of these stages either as a participant or an observer and it is important that you record the status of your experience on the PEDR form. The RIBA advises practices as to what activities should be participatory and which should be observed, although offices do not necessarily strictly adhere to the recommendations.

**Recording Project Details**

The PEDR form also requires a brief description of the projects on which you are working. The information you would provide within this category includes: the title of the project (e.g. house extension/clinic), its general location (e.g. North London/Maidstone, Kent), its size (e.g. 60, 60,000 sqm), the client (e.g. private commission or a public one, say the Kent Regional Health Authority) and the budget (e.g. £80,000/12 million). You are also required to indicate a summary of the number of hours completed per work stage for each project and state whether you were a participant or an observer. You are also strongly recommended to keep a portfolio record of the project(s) on which you are working, in particular focusing on the drawings, models and photographic/digital record of the specific work undertaken *by you* during this period. This tends to be invaluable when applying for a place on a Part 2 course, when applying for post-Part 2 experience placements and part of your "documentary submission" when you take your Part 3 examinations.

### Recording Project Commentaries

You will also be required to complete a commentary on your experience. The questions you need to respond to include:

1. What do you think you have learnt from your experience over the past 3 months?
2. How would you evaluate your performance?
3. What do you aim to achieve over the next 3 months?
4. What additional skills do you need to develop, or experience gained, in order to achieve the above?
5. Any other comments?

This part of the record is most useful if you approach it as a self-appraisal. It offers the opportunity for you to reflect on your experience to date, to think about what you are hoping and aiming to do, and what action may be needed from yourself, your Employment Mentor or Professional Advisor to ensure that your experience is as valuable as possible.

### Getting Signatures

The record is then signed and dated by yourself, your Employment Mentor and your Professional Advisor. You will need to get the appropriate signatures every 3 months. This period is long enough to allow you to build up enough experience, but also short enough for you to address any gaps with your advisor and mentor.

### Ensuring Balance and Quality

The quality of your experience will depend, of course, on the practice for which you work, the opportunities you are offered and the type of person you are, your skills and ability to take up challenges. Your Employment Mentor, however, does have an obligation to try and ensure that your experience is as diverse and educational as possible.

Your Professional Advisor can also be of help here, in providing guidance both to you and your employer, advising on a wide range of areas affecting your employment from pay and conditions to the variety and quality of your experience. Your advisor and mentor both have a responsibility to check and sign your PEDR, and should comment on both the scope and complexity of your experience.

They can both advise your employers on the abilities a student architect will be expected to have at any point during their training and will advise you and your employer should your training not be of a breadth and standard required by the ARB and RIBA.

Your Professional Advisor can also help you negotiate your employment conditions. However, the advisor's role is, as the name suggests, only advisory, she/he cannot "interfere" with your experience in a practice and the level of support given by an advisor varies enormously from school to school. It is also important to note that although architect employers have a legal responsibility as far as pay and conditions are concerned, they are not *legally bound* to provide you with the experience necessary to pass Part 3.[10] In this respect, you are relying on the goodwill of the profession and should you and your Professional Advisor, having attempted to correct matters with an unhelpful employer, find that your experience is inadequate, you should find alternative employment.

The quality and diversity of your practical experience depends primarily on the office in which you find work. At its best it will give you the opportunity to experience and understand at first hand the many duties and responsibilities of an architect, how offices work, the processes of design, the tendering process and construction, contract management and the potential range of opportunities and career directions an architect may take. At worst, however, you may find yourself doing repetitive and unchallenging work.

Remember that everyone may have to take a turn making the tea or coffee when working in a practice, but you should start to question the situation if this is still your main function 1 month into your professional training. In an ideal world, in the course of your 24 months of professional experience, you would gain experience in all the responsibilities and duties of an architect, although ultimately it is the *job of the qualified architect you are working under to take final responsibility for anything you are instructed to undertake.*

---

[10]However, a new RIBA template at www.pedr.co.uk, which sets out requirements for "professional experience employment contracts" at Stages 1 and 2 may prove helpful with its emphasis on mutual obligation, professionalism, and fair treatment of student and graduate employees.

### The Employment Mentor

When you start work in a practice, your role will be to act as an assistant to a qualified architect who may also be your Employment Mentor. An introduction to this person should be expected on your first day in the office, unless there are unavoidable circumstances, in which case you should be told which architect has been assigned to you to act as your Employment Mentor and when you will be able to meet them.

If this does not happen (wait a week or so), you should speak to a senior member of the practice to ensure that this is not overlooked. Your Employment Mentor is a vital person in your professional experience. She/he has a duty to try and ensure that you gain the best experience that you can. Nonetheless, as already stated, the quality of your experience does necessarily depend on the type of practice, the projects it has while you work there and on the overall breadth, depth and balance of experience you get in a number of offices. The range and types of offices you work for are therefore central to the experience you gain during your 24 months of professional work. If you consider the year out as a foundation to Professional Practice, then doing your best to gain constructive and challenging experience is obviously of huge significance to your career. If this does not happen within your first 3 months in an office, and you have a choice (i.e. the economy is good enough) move on. Although it will not be the end of the world if things fall short of your ambition at this stage, a proactive and assertive response to the challenge of both finding and "using" a good year-out position is strongly recommended.

Ultimately, it is the Part 3 examiners who decide whether your experience and level of competence entitles you to become an architect. If there are any doubts about the nature of your year out experience, even if you appear to have adhered to the rules laid out by ARB/RIBA, you may fail your examination. If you have more unusual experience, say working for a firm other than an architectural practice, you should get advice from your Professional Advisor to ensure that their work will be a legitimate experience contributing to your Part 3 examination.

### The Code of Conduct

When employed within a practice as an architectural assistant, it is your Employment Mentor's responsibility to ensure that you are not given duties beyond your level of qualification or maturity. Nonetheless, just as those around you will have a responsibility to ensure that you have a useful and broad experience during your year out, there will be requirements you will need to fulfil. Most important of these will be your compliance with the Code of Conduct set by the RIBA. Unlike the ARB's Code of Conduct, which is applicable to all registered architects only, the RIBA Code applies to both architects and students of architecture. The code outlines the dedication, integrity, responsibilities, loyalty to your employer and professionalism in everyday practice required of an architect or student of architecture. Some aspects of the code of course do not apply to students; for example, until you are registered you are not required to carry Personal Indemnity Insurance. The code does, however, require a level of professionalism and responsibility in the architectural student. Any behaviour that is seen as unacceptable to the profession may prevent you from passing Part 3 and therefore barring you from registering as an architect at the end of your education. The full version of the RIBA Code of Conduct can be found at the RIBA web site.

### Getting Help

As discussed earlier, both your Employment Mentor and Professional Advisor are given guidance from the RIBA as to what you should be doing in the office during your year out. Anyone can access this information by visiting the RIBA PEDR web site and it would be advisable for you to know what advice and guidelines they are using. This will enable you to be reasonable, informed, and constructive when discussing your experience and future plans. Despite this guidance, however, the involvement that a school of architecture will have with any of its pupils depends on the particular school and varies enormously. If you do some research you will find that some schools get very involved from helping students to get a job in the first place (helping them prepare a curriculum vitae (CV), making contacts and so on) to visiting them in their place of work and discussing their progress and experience with the student's Employment Mentor. Other schools have almost no contact with their students whilst working: again find out what the minimum requirement is as established by the RIBA and then discuss any shortcomings with both parties.

## Finally: Preparing for Part 3 of the Professional Examination

Preparing for Part 3 of the Professional Examination itself is demanding and can be stressful, as you will most likely be in a full-time job at the time, and will have to prepare for the examination in your spare time. Most Professional Practice and Management courses ask you to prepare case studies based on your office work as well, so you will be busy. Nonetheless, such study should be viewed as an extension of your working practice in the office. All jobs being run in your employer's practice will be relevant to the Part 3 syllabus and the experience of your colleagues and the job files will be an excellent source of information in your understanding of the profession. Remember, all the qualified architects in your office have been through this process. You should be very careful not to harass busy people for information, but politely requesting to look at job files or asking specific questions about current or past projects will usually be okay within the office environment.

The RIBA Part 3 syllabus can be viewed in full at www.pedr.co.uk/empout.asp and your preparation for the examination can start early in your career. Your diary and PEDR can be used as a continuous professional journal where you record any information or experience that may be relevant. By knowing the Part 3 syllabus you will be in a better position to make relevant and useful notes and observations. Make sure that you stay in touch with fellow students, share research tasks, and revise together. Different schools of architecture have different formats for the examination, but all will involve a personal interview, so verbal preparation is also very important, as is presenting yourself professionally, down to how you dress for the interview. If your Part 3 Professional Examination preparation course does not do this, work with fellow students in preparing and sitting mock written and verbal examinations. The pass rate in the professional examination varies a lot, so do not be demoralized if you fail the first time. On the other hand, there is no reason, if your professional experience record is strong and you have prepared thoroughly, that you should not pass.

The RIBA recognizes that there are certain circumstances where the PEDR is not an appropriate record of experience. This may be the case for non-UK architects or mature students with lengthy experience within the profession who want to apply to be registered as practising architects in the UK. In these circumstances you may apply to the RIBA to use Certificate of Professional Experience instead of the PEDR (a system based on employer certification of your professional experience over a longer period), although this is dependent on you satisfying the following conditions. That is, you:

- must be over 30 years old;
- must have a minimum of 6 years of experience in architects' offices;
- must be working at a sufficient level to be capable of taking responsibility for small jobs or of acting as a team leader in charge of a number of assistants engaged on either a large project or a series of smaller projects;
- have not been able, for reasons considered valid by the Professional Studies Advisor, to maintain a PEDR.

The RIBA requires the Certificate of Professional Experience to be signed by your employer, who must be a principal in private practice or the chief architect in a public commercial or industrial practice. A separate certificate must be submitted for each separate period of employment. You will be required to submit a Certificate of Professional Experience instead of, or as an extension to, the PEDR when applying for the RIBA Examination in Professional Practice and Management (Part 3).

## How a Foreign Architect Can Apply to Register as a UK Architect

If you are qualified as an architect in a country other than the UK or EU, you can apply to register to practice in the UK by the following method. First you should obtain application forms from the ARB for an individual assessment of your architectural qualifications. If you meet the necessary first stage criteria, the ARB will invite you to attend an oral examination. You will meet with a panel of 3 UK registered architects who will assess your portfolio and discuss your education and projects to establish equivalence to the Part 1 and Part 2 stages of UK architectural education. This process is also accepted by the RIBA for professional membership requirements.

The process is rigorous and it is important that you prepare well. It is advisable to begin preparations by compiling an extensive and detailed CV, which you can use as the structure for your portfolio. The latter should demonstrate a good cross-section of your architectural education, skills, experience, and abilities as a practising architect. Where possible you should include exemplary work from your university architecture course, supported by work from practice and in particular examples of buildings which demonstrate your skills as a designer and project manager. Include a variety of media, project diaries and any examples of work that you have had published. The ARB and RIBA will be interested in the diversity and extent of your skills – make sure you include examples of as broad a range of projects as you can. Be prepared to discuss your work and experience in detail and always be honest about any gaps in your knowledge or experience. Of particular concern will be your ability to integrate your technical expertise into high-quality design projects, sensitivity to context and urban design and an understanding of the principles of sustainable design.

The Assessment Panel has the power to grant you recognition for Parts 1 and 2. If you gain this, you are then required to attend a validated course at a School of Architecture leading to the RIBA Examination in

Professional Practice and Management (Part 3). The content and structure of these courses vary and you should study each school's Part 3 syllabus with care, discussing any queries with the school's Professional Advisor to ensure that, where possible, you embark on a course of study that is best for your experience and interest.

As already stated in this chapter, the content and focus of courses at different schools of architecture within the UK vary hugely, but standards are equal across them. Your experience and ability will be judged against this benchmark and it is therefore wise to do some research into work produced at Parts 1 and 2 in schools in the UK. You can do this from a distance by visiting the list of validated courses on www.pedr.co.uk and then the individual Schools' web sites. Some schools maintain excellent, regularly updated web sites where you can view exhibitions of best work, past end of year catalogues, prize winners' work and so on. You can also, of course, visit end of year exhibitions, the locations and dates of which are advertised in *Building Design*.

You may find that the Assessment Panel recommend to the ARB and RIBA that you be recognized for equivalence to one or both of Parts 1 and 2. It is often the case that architects educated outside of the UK have not experienced the type of study necessary for UK registration and RIBA professional membership. In this case, the best course of action, should you wish to continue on your quest for UK registration, is to study at an undergraduate/graduate programme at a validated school of architecture in the UK. You may in fact find that your experience and skills can be used to gain credit for some parts of the course. This might mean exemption from a particular module, but could mean as much as exemption from 1 to 2 years of an undergraduate 3-year degree. The amount of credit you can gain may vary from school to school. You will need to research well and talk to a school's Admissions tutor or Professional Advisor to establish how much exemption you may be eligible to gain at that particular institution.

## A Final Note

Remember: whether you are a potential student of architecture or well on the way to becoming fully qualified, you are at just one stage of an exciting, challenging, and rewarding career. By taking some time to plan and take control of your professional experience, you will be making huge strides in your career development. Good Luck!

# 6 Internship and Beyond: Becoming an Architect in the USA

In this chapter you will learn about the Internship Development Program (IDP), an important part of the process that leads to architectural registration in the USA. We will also introduce two legal bodies that are involved in shaping the guidelines for architectural education and professional experience in the USA that lead up to registration as an architect: the National Council of Architectural Registration Boards (NCARB), and the American Institute of Architects (AIA).

## The National Council of Architectural Registration Boards

In order to register and practice as an architect in the USA, it is necessary to comply with the requirements of the National Council of Architectural Registration Boards (NCARB). NCARB is a non-profit corporation, composed of all legally constituted Boards of Architecture in the 50 states of the nation, plus the District of Columbia, Guam, the Northern Mariana Islands, Puerto Rico, and the USA Virgin Islands. Each of these Boards has the final authority to decide who will be given a license to practice architecture within that Board's jurisdiction. Please note that the term "license" is also known as "registration", and that these two terms mean the same thing.

The architectural license/registration is "one of the means by which the US registration boards fulfil their mission to safeguard public health, safety, and welfare".[1] It is also important to understand that NCARB is a federation of Boards of Architecture, and therefore also acts as a group to collectively recommend various standards for licensing, ranging from the content of education and internship, to the nature of continuing education of architects. Although standards in individual states may not be adopted nationally, the majority of Boards have adopted similar standards for registration, thus enabling greater consistency of requirements for initial registration and reciprocal registration between different states within the USA. Many of NCARB's requirements are also compatible with those of the Committee of Canadian Architectural Councils (CCAC), offering avenues for reciprocal registration between the two countries.

This chapter outlines current NCARB requirements for internship and registration, available at the time of publication of this book. For more information on NCARB, its responsibilities, activities, and legislation, and to check whether the information we offer you here has changed, you should visit their web site at www.ncarb.org

## American Institute of Architects

The American Institute of Architects (AIA) is an institute whose membership represents the architectural profession before and beyond the registration process. It acts as "the voice of the architecture profession dedicated to: serving its members, advancing their value, and improving the quality of the built environment".[2] The vision statement of the AIA states that "through a culture of innovation, The American Institute of Architects empowers its members and inspires creation of a better built environment".[3] With more than 70,000 members, the AIA is a professional institute, providing advisory and information services for its members, and supporting them in their day-to-day practice of architecture. Like the Royal Institute of British Architects (RIBA), the AIA upholds The Code of Ethics and Professional Conduct that applies to the professional activities of all its members. The requirements of the code are similar to those of the RIBA

---

[1] *ARE Guidelines Version 3.0* (Washington, DC: NCARB, 2004); p. 1.
[2] For more information about the AIA, its governing bodies, mission statement, membership, and activities, visit http://www.aia.org. You can also obtain more information by contacting the AIA at: The American Institute of Architects, 1735 New York Avenue, NW, Washington, DC 20006-5292, telephone: 800-AIA-3837 or 202-626-7300, facsimile: 202-626-7547, e-mail: infocentral@aia.org.
[3] http://www.aia.org

and failure to comply may result in disciplinary action by the AIA. Conformity to the Code of Ethics and Professional Conduct is a central part of being a registered architect in the USA and it is important that you familiarize yourself with it before you enter the internship experience. The AIA does not, however, have direct control of the registration/licensing process.

## The Establishment and Monitoring of Professional Qualifications

The gaining of qualifications and practical experience in the USA is, as in the UK, strictly controlled by five architectural organizations. These include of NCARB and the AIA (both described above), and the NAAB (National Architectural Accrediting Board, described below). In addition, AIAS (American Institute of Architecture Students) and the ACSA (Association of Collegiate Schools of Architecture) are involved in the process of accrediting professional architectural education. These organizations work together to ensure that agreed standards are upheld at every level of education and practice, both by students of architecture, architectural interns, and registered architects. NCARB, via its member registration boards, establishes and maintains the standards for registration of architects. AIA membership, unlike registration, is optional. However, unlike the RIBA, the AIA does not act as a sole agent to validate or accredit architectural education. There are currently over 100 schools of architecture in the USA with accredited professional programmes. Schools of architecture can have 2-, 3- or 6-year accreditation periods, with 6 years being the most favourable. It is therefore important that you verify that the programme of your choice is accredited by NAAB if you intend to become registered to practice architecture.

## Becoming a Registered Architect in the USA: The Basics

The path to becoming a registered architect in the USA involves four steps: education, internship, examination, and registration. Under normal circumstances, to become registered to practice architecture in the USA, an applicant would undertake and successfully achieve the following:

(i) Completion of an architectural degree programme accredited by the NAAB. Some states will allow a pre-professional degree in architecture with an additional internship period to be the equivalent of an accredited degree. The education requirements of each state can change abruptly, so you must check with your state registration board to make sure you will meet that state's current stipulations.

(ii) Successful completion of the training requirements of the Internship Development Program (IDP).
(iii) Passing the Architectural Registration Examination (ARE).
(iv) Completion of an application for registration as an architect in one of the states or jurisdictions under NCARB's control.

In many states, to maintain one's architectural registration, an architect also needs to undertake continuing education, which needs to occur at a minimum on a yearly basis.

Since the internship process, or the IDP, is the primary focus of this chapter, we will not discuss NCARB "Certification" or continuing education here in any depth. We advise you to contact NCARB if you wish to know more about these two topics.

### The Education Process

The architectural education process is intended to ensure and examine a student's competence in the skills necessary to become an independent practising architect. In order to fulfil the educational requirements to practise architecture, students typically must earn a professional degree from an architectural programme accredited by the NAAB. There are three main types of architectural programmes that may lead to registration as an architect: a 4-year B.A. or B.S. in Architectural Studies (these degrees are not accredited by NAAB), the professional 5-year Bachelor of Architecture (B.Arch.) degree and the professional Master of Architecture (M.Arch.) degree.

Thirty-five of the 55 NCARB jurisdictions which confer registration to practice architecture require a degree from one of the two types of professional degree programme, that is, either a B.Arch. or an M.Arch. degree. The other 20 NCARB jurisdictions currently accept a B.S. or B.A. pre-professional degree in architecture. Interestingly, states that accept this degree are among those with the largest number of registered architects: California, New York, and Illinois. The chart below lists the states that require each type of degree at the time of the first publication of this book:

---

States which require an accredited B.Arch. or M.Arch. degree

| | | | |
|---|---|---|---|
| Alabama | Alaska | Arkansas | Connecticut |
| Delaware | District of Columbia | Florida | Indiana |
| Iowa | Kansas | Kentucky | Louisiana |
| Massachusetts | Michigan | Minnesota | Mississippi |

| Montana | Nebraska | Nevada | New Jersey |
|---------|----------|--------|------------|
| New Mexico | North Carolina | North Dakota | Ohio |
| Oklahoma | Oregon | Pennsylvania | Puerto Rico |
| Rhode Island | South Carolina | South Dakota | Utah |
| Virginia | West Virginia | Wyoming | |

States which do not require an accredited degree (many require a B.A. or B.S. in Architectural Studies)

| Arizona | California | Colorado | Georgia |
|---------|-----------|----------|---------|
| Guam | Hawaii | Idaho | Illinois |
| Maine | Maryland | Missouri | New Hampshire |
| New York | Northern Mariana Islands | Tennessee | Texas |
| Vermont | Virgin Islands | Washington | Wisconsin |

Registration requirements for each board can be found at http://www.ncarb.org/stateboards/index.html.

The NAAB (www.naab.org) web site offers an updated list of accredited programmes in architecture, which can help you to find out if your desired programme qualifies you for architectural registration in most states. It is normal for students who take the 4-year pre-professional architecture degree in one institution to continue at another institution to complete an M.Arch. degree. Some of these architectural programmes integrate professional experience into the curriculum, while others do not. We highly recommend that you research the different options offered by different schools so as to gain the best advantage when seeking an internship position.

Within each professional programme, the areas of architectural education prescribed by NAAB include:

- general education (English, mathematics, the humanities, and the social and natural sciences);
- architectural history, human behaviour and environment;
- architectural design;
- structural design;
- technical systems (mechanical, electrical, plumbing and fire protection systems for buildings, materials and methods of construction, life safety systems, and accessibility design;
- practice (business and practice management, contracts, cost estimating and finance, laws, and governmental regulations).

*Variations*

Part-Time Studies

Some schools in the USA offer part-time architectural education. The best known of these are the Boston Architectural Center, and the New School of Architecture & Design in San Diego, which allow their students to hold full-time jobs and attend classes in the evenings and on weekends. Of course, this option means that the time taken to accumulate education credits is much longer than usual, but it does have the advantage of ensuring that at the completion of formal education the student has a good chance of having completed the internship training requirements.

Foreign Educational Qualifications

Education outside the USA may not include all of the above components, or such components may not be easily separable in a transcript of educational qualifications. If you have graduated from a foreign architectural school, you should have your educational credentials identified and categorized through a process called the Education Evaluation Services for Architects (EESA). This process is administered by the NAAB (www.naab.org). Your educational credentials are evaluated by EESA educator evaluators, who identify the areas of your compliance or deficiency in meeting the defined educational standard. In case of an identified educational deficiency, you will then proceed to fulfil the requirements as prescribed by the EESA evaluators.

## IDP

To be eligible for the ARE, you must complete a specified period of training through the IDP. The IDP, like the ARE, is a national programme and its primary goal is to help trainee professionals in their transition from academia to practice. It is, essentially, an apprenticeship system, that ensures you get the kind of experience you need to learn the broad responsibilities of an architect, and helps you to get ready to take the ARE.

Although the IDP did not officially begin until 1978, the history of apprenticeship and mentorship in architecture dates back to a time before schools of architecture were established. From the Middle Ages onwards experienced master builders and later architects took on apprentices to teach them basics of architectural practice. In a way, these roots speak of a common origin for both architectural academia and practice – a world of learning for young professionals that combines the classroom, construction site, and office experience into a single learning process. This traditional model of mentorship waned with the increasing responsibilities of a master architect and complexities of the architectural profession, as well as changes in production created by the growing division of labour of the capitalist economy, and the growth of specialized interests that created the architectural profession, as we know it today.

Architectural schools emerged in the nineteenth century to address both growing job specialization and the need to formalize professional knowledge, and began to compete with the apprenticeship model. However, young and inexperienced graduates of the newly formed architectural schools were not yet ready to take on the full responsibility of a professional architect, and still had to rely on an experienced professional to provide a first-hand advice and exposure to all the complexities of an increasingly demanding profession.

The transitional period from academia to practice and the ability to apply the knowledge and skills acquired in school became the focus of many registration boards. Various attempts were made over the years to structure this transitional period, or internship as it is most commonly known in the USA. The definition of what constituted the most appropriate length and content of an internship varied considerably among the member boards of NCARB. In the mid-1970s, in response to the many different internship requirements across the nation, the IDP emerged, aiming to provide structured practical experience with a clear definition and prescribed path for its successful accomplishment. The programme was initiated by four collateral organizations – AIA, ACSA, AIAS, and NCARB – organizations that today continue to sponsor the IDP, its policies and procedures. Outlined in this chapter are the IDP training requirements.

*Important Reminder*

Before we go into more detail about IDP training requirements, it is important to remind you that, as with all other information, these requirements are subject to a constant change. We will give you much useful advice below, which we hope will help you take best advantage of what the IDP program has to offer, but you should also always consult the NCARB web site (www.ncarb.org) to make sure you know exactly what you need to do. You should carefully compare the guidelines to the criteria established by the particular state registration board in which you intend to take the licensing examination and practice architecture, because these can differ from state to state. The NCARB web site is very useful, not only for information about the IDP program, but also about the many other aspects of architectural practice in the USA.

Useful IDP Resources available on the Internet:

- AIA resources for IDP: www.aia.org/idp/idpresources.asp;
- NCARB resources for IDP: www.ncarb.org/idp/resources.htm;
- AIA State Components: www.aia.org/institute/chapters;
- IDP State Coordinators and IDP Educator Coordinators: www.aia.org/idp/coordroster.asp

*General Rules: Time*

When Does Internship Experience Begin?

It is important to understand that you can start earning training credit (IDP "training units") before you graduate. However, NCARB defines that *no* training units may be earned prior to the satisfactory completion of:

- 3 years in an NAAB- or Canadian Architectural Certification Board (CACB)-accredited professional degree programme;
- the third year of a 4-year pre-professional degree programme in architecture accepted for direct entry to an NAAB- or CACB-accredited professional degree programme;
- 1 year in an NAAB- or CACB-accredited M.Arch. degree programme for interns with undergraduate degrees in another discipline;
- 96 semester credit hours as evaluated by EESA in accordance with NCARB's Education Requirement, of which no more than 60 hours can be in the general education subject area.[4]

This does not mean that you cannot begin to work in an architectural firm earlier, and it may be useful for your personal development (and sometimes for your pocket as well) to do so. However, you will not be able to count this experience as IDP credit. You can count part-time and summer work once you have fulfilled the requirements above, but should

---

[4]For purposes of calculating years of education, 32 semester or 48 quarter credit hours shall equal 1 year in an academic programme. It is important to understand that not all states have adopted the NCARB education and training standards.

know that often the quality of professional experience in a part-time or summer position is not as good as in a full-time year-long contract, simply because you cannot see a building through much of its procurement process.

## How to begin the process

After you have successfully completed your education requirements (whether the minimum periods outlined above, or the completion of a full pre-professional or professional degree programme), and once you have gained a position in the architectural workforce, you are ready to start documenting your progress in the IDP. First, you should contact your state registration board to make sure you have all the information you need about the IDP process (see below). Much of this information is on the NCARB web site, but it is useful to call NCARB as well to make sure you understand everything correctly before you begin.

### General Rules: Supervision

#### Working for an Architect Registered in the USA

The controlled nature of becoming and practising as an architect in the USA means that the main part of your internship experience has to occur under the supervision of an architect registered in the USA, working in a practice engaged in a comprehensive range of architectural services. Most architecture interns gain their IDP experience in conventional architectural offices under the supervision of a registered architect, but others may spend some time working for a contractor, engineer, landscape architect, or other type of practice as outlined in Chapter 3.

#### The Supervisor

The IDP supervisor is an architect who must hold a current licence in the state where she/he practices architecture. This is the person that supervises your work at the office, someone who is familiar with your day-to-day activities and assignments, and will verify and sign your NCARB employment verification/IDP training unit report forms. As you can imagine, it is better to select a supervisor who is familiar with the IDP process and can answer questions as they arise. You will need your supervisor to make sure that you are learning the right things and learning them the right way. As in the UK, when you start work in an architectural firm, you will normally work under the direct supervision of a qualified architect who may also be your IDP supervisor. You should expect to be introduced to your supervisor on your first day in the office, unless there are unavoidable circumstances (e.g. sickness), in which case you should be told which architect has been assigned to you and when you will be able to meet them. It is ideal if your supervisor at the office is someone with influence in the firm. This is important because one of the tasks of your supervisor is to help you get as broad a range of experience as possible to satisfy IDP requirements, and that may mean being involved in activities that may lie outside the project to which you have been assigned. Your supervisor does not have to be a partner or principal in the firm. It is very important that she/he is licensed, and it is very helpful if she/he is the project architect of the main project with which you are associated, so that she/he can help you get as good a range of experience on that project as possible. The supervisor should have a close working knowledge of what you are working on, so as to make sure that you are getting not only the breadth, but also the depth of experience that you need. Your supervisor will be required to sign your IDP Training Unit Report Form.

### The Mentor

In addition to having a supervisor, you should also select a mentor, a person who will meet with you at least once a month to review your IDP training progress. The mentor is there to help you set and clarify your broader career objectives. Like your supervisor, a mentor must hold a current architectural license; however, and unlike the supervisor, she/he does not have to be registered in the state where your firm or organization is located. Since your mentor provides broader career guidance from a perspective that should be objective, confidential, and independent from your current employment, most interns select a mentor from outside their current office. Although you can elect to have your supervisor serve as your mentor, it is wise to broaden your networks and look for a different person – whether within your office or outside it. The NCARB web site also states that "for all training occurring after July 1, 2000 your IDP mentor must sign to acknowledge your IDP Training Unit Report".[5] It is important to understand that a mentor might have a

---

[5]http://www.ncarb.org/idp/gettingstarted.htm

significant impact on your career through guidance, advice, intellectual support, and in some cases lifelong friendship. You can select a mentor through an informal process, such as through discussions with your supervisor, faculty members, or fellow interns. You can also request formal assistance from the AIA or your local IDP coordinator (http://www.aia.org/idp/coordroster.asp), who can help you identify professionals in your area who have volunteered to serve as mentors to recent graduates. Either way, make sure that you select someone who is motivating, inspiring, cares about your professional career, and above all, is a good listener.

*Council Record and IDP Workbook*

After selecting your supervisor and your mentor, you are ready to establish a record of your IDP activities. The NCARB Council Record is the official record of your qualifications and experience that NCARB uses to evaluate your eligibility to take the ARE. The Council Record comprises your educational transcripts and your employment verification/IDP training unit report forms. Between these two categories of information you should find that all your educational and practical experience is covered. In order to initiate your NCARB Council Record, you must request an application form from

NCARB
1801 K Street, NW, Suite 1100-K
Washington
DC 20006

If you wish to do this more quickly, you can download all the necessary forms from the NCARB web site and mail them together with the application fee to the address above. Once it has received your payment and application form, NCARB will acknowledge your application and send you requests for transcripts and employment verification/IDP training unit report forms. You will then be responsible for preparing and sending these forms to your architecture school (or schools, if you have attended more than one), and to your employer (or employers, if you have worked in more than one firm during periods of eligibility for the IDP). These forms must be completed by an authorized person at those institutions and returned directly to NCARB so that your Council Record can be established. Once it is set up, it is important to know that you can constantly monitor the status of your Council Record through the

NCARB web site. The process of establishing a Council Record takes time – be prepared for it to take up to 6 months – and it is possible that some of your experience or even a part of your education may not be accepted, so do not expect to take the ARE the moment you have decided you are ready.

The IDP Training Unit Workbook is a digital tool you can download from the NCARB web site that you should use for recording your experience on a daily basis. In most offices you will, in any case, be keeping a record of your hours which will be billable to a client – you can transfer this information easily to the Training Unit Workbook, which will simply require you to add a category of work to describe the nature of your training experience. As well as documenting what you do, this process should help identify "weak training areas", which you can then discuss with your supervisor and request assignments to give you a greater exposure to those (weak or under-represented) areas. The IDP Training Unit Workbook also represents an easy way of preparing accurate IDP Training Unit Reports for submission to NCARB. To download and access information about the IDP Training Unit Workbook visit http://www.ncarb.org/idp/idpworkbook.html

*IDP Training Categories*

The IDP defines four training categories of architectural practice in which interns must acquire experience. You must complete 700 training units to satisfy the IDP training requirement, bearing in mind that one training unit equals 8 hours of acceptable activity in a given training area. This adds up to almost three years of training. There is no strict limit as to how much chronological time it might take you to complete your IDP, but the sooner you are exposed to all the aspects of architectural practice (or project phases), the sooner you will be able to fulfil particular experience requirements. The four required training categories[6] are as follows:

- Design and Construction Documents (Category A)
- Construction Administration (Category B)
- Management (Category C)
- Related Activities, including Professional and Community Service (Category D)

---

[6] *Intern Development Program Guidelines 2003–2004* (Washington, DC: NCARB, 2003); p. 20B.

Each of the IDP training categories is subdivided into training areas. These are briefed below.[7]

Category A: Design and Construction Documents

| Training areas | Minimum training units required |
|---|---|
| 1. Programming | 10 |
| 2. Site and environmental analysis | 10 |
| 3. Schematic design | 15 |
| 4. Engineering systems coordination | 15 |
| 5. Building cost analysis | 10 |
| 6. Code research | 15 |
| 7. Design development | 40 |
| 8. Construction documents | 135 |
| 9. Specifications and materials research | 15 |
| 10. Documents checking and coordination | 10 |
| Total | 275 |
| Total training units required in training areas | 350 |

As you can see, the total number of units in Category A (350) includes the minimum of 275 required units, plus 75 additional training units that must be earned in any of the training areas 1–10. That gives you some flexibility to focus on a particular area you enjoy or find interesting. For example, site and environmental analysis can provide an opportunity to research the social or ecological context of the site for your project, and schematic design offers an opportunity to use your design and visual communication skills to evolve design alternatives for a project. If an office is willing to cover the cost of your time for these types of investigations, you may find yourself with some interesting research or design work indeed. If an office does not have the resources (few clients like to pay for research activity) then you may well take some unpaid time to do so, particularly if it involves you gaining very marketable skills, such as knowledge of the building code, specifications, and materials. Much of such learning can be very enjoyable. For example, a visit to a factory or shop to understand the making of building components counts as materials research and can teach you an enormous amount about the advantages and disadvantages of a particular building material or component.

---

[7]http://www.ncarb.org/IDP/idptraining.htm

Category B: Construction Administration

| Training areas | Minimum training units required |
| --- | --- |
| 11.  Bidding and contract negotiation | 10 |
| 12.  Construction phase office | 15 |
| 13.  Construction phase observation | 15 |
| Total | 40 |
| Total training units required | 70 |

The total of 70 units in this category includes the 40 minimum training units required (subcategories 11–13), plus 30 additional training units that must be earned in any of the training areas 11–13. This is one of the harder areas in which to get experience as an intern, but it is a critical one, so persist in asking if you find that your office prefers to give such work only to more senior employees. Ask to be included as an addition to senior employees, so you can see how they handle the bidding process and how they communicate with contractors in the process of reaching an appropriate contract cost. Learning how to negotiate contracts is an important skill, and is not learned overnight, so ask to be included many times. Try to participate in the observation of construction as regularly as you can – not only for the sake of the IDP process, but because seeing things being built, and asking skilled construction professionals why they work the way they do, is the best way to understand construction. You will be amazed by how many construction professionals will take time to explain a construction technique to an intern, especially if it is in an area of the job where you were not involved in the production of construction documentation. Here, also, ask your supervisor as much as you can, so that you can learn from their experience.

Category C: Management

| Training areas | Minimum training units required |
| --- | --- |
| 14.  Project management | 15 |
| 15.  Office management | 10 |
| Elective units in this category | 10 |
| Total training units required | 35 |

The management of a project may not, at first, seem a compelling or complex aspect of being an architect. However, understanding how information production needs to be phased, and who the best people are that can do this, can make or break an architectural office. A mis-managed flow of information, produced by people who are not appro-priately prepared, can lead to huge cost overruns and claims. Just as there are elegant and efficient ways to assemble materials, so there are elegant and efficient ways to assemble information and teams that make it. Even in a small, one-person project, the appropriate phasing of work can make the difference between a happy contractor and client, and deep frustration.

Category D: Related Activities

| Training areas | Minimum training units required |
|---|---|
| 16. Professional and community service | 10 |
| 17. Other related activities | 0 |
| Total training units required | 10 |

While this area only contains 10 units, or 80 hours of work, it offers some interesting possibilities. Professional and community service allows you the opportunity to become active in your local AIA chapter or to use your fledgling architectural expertise to serve the needs of a community, say in helping to organize a community garden, or run a community design charrette, or supporting community activism in zoning disputes.

*The Total Package*

| | |
|---|---|
| Total IDP training units required in areas above | 465 |
| Total IDP training units required | 700 |

In order to fully satisfy IDP training requirements, a specifically prescribed period of training must be completed in each of the 16 training areas. If you add all four categories A–D, you will see that combined they only require a minimum of 465 training units. However, you still need to earn a total of 700 units. This means that the additional 235 training units may be acquired in any of the categories, which gives you yet more flexibility and opportunity to build up a particular slant or specialization. For example, if you wish to pursue your passion for ecological research, you can spend all of your remaining 235 training units on that, or on working with a community, or doing architectural competitions, or working for a real estate developer, or learning about construction by building. The one critical thing to remember is that all this must be done under the supervision of a qualified professional in an appropriate firm – not all offices will meet the criteria that will allow you full flexibility with your training units. To understand whether an office can provide appropriate supervision of your work, you also need to understand IDP requirements for training settings.

*Training Settings*

The purpose of *training settings* is to ensure that the majority of your experience is obtained under the supervision of an architect whose work is subject to the construction, management and legal constraints, practices and knowledge in the USA. When selecting your future employer, it is therefore important to carefully screen the kind of practice in which a particular office is engaged. You can do so by checking the firm's web site and making sure that architecture is their primary activity. If it is not, you should check at the interview if you will be able to work with a registered architect.

In addition to defining the acceptable training settings, NCARB defines the maximum number of units that you can earn in a certain type of practice or under the supervision of a certain type of registered and/or non-registered individual. For example, there is no limit as to how many units you can earn if you are training under the direct supervision of a person who is a *registered architect, and* when the organization encompasses the comprehensive practice of architecture, including each of the IDP training areas.

A *registered architect* is a person registered to practice architecture in the jurisdiction (state) in which they practice. According to the NCARB's web site, "direct supervision means that degree of supervision by a person overseeing the work of another, where both work in the same office in circumstances where personal contact is routine, whereby the supervisor has both control over and detailed professional knowledge of the work prepared under his or her supervision".[8] For the purpose of this book, we will label the instance in the preceding paragraph as a training setting 1, and label other trainings settings as 2, 3, 4, 5, 6, and 7. Please note that

---

[8]http://www.ncarb.org/idp/trainingsettings.htm

these are not official NCARB numbers, but our attempt to make the classifications more accessible to international readers, and especially to make a clear distinction between the names of the training categories defined by NCARB (A–D) and the training settings defined by us (1–7).

NCARB limits the maximum number of training units that you can earn in training settings 2–7 as follows:

- *Training setting 2*: If you are practising under supervision of a person who is a registered architect, but the company does *not* encompass the comprehensive practice of architecture, then you can earn a maximum of 465 training units.
- *Training setting 3*: If you are training in a firm that practices architecture abroad (outside the USA or Canada), under the direct supervision of a person practising architecture, who is not registered in a US or a Canadian jurisdiction, then you can earn a maximum of 235 training units.
- *Training setting 4*: If you are training and gaining experience directly related to architecture under the direct supervision of a registered landscape architect and/or a registered engineer (structural, civil, mechanical, or electrical engineer in the field of building construction), then you can earn a maximum of 235 training units in training categories B–D; as a consequence, you will need to earn your units in training category A (design and construction documents) under training settings 1, 2, or 3.
- *Training setting 5*: If you are gaining experience (other than that in training settings 1–4) under the direct supervision of a person who is experienced in the design and construction of the built environment, but not a registered professional, then you can earn a maximum of 117 training units in training categories C and D; as a consequence, you will need to earn your units in training categories A (design and construction documents) and B (construction administration) when employed in training settings 1, 2, or 3.
- *Training setting 6*: If you are teaching full-time or conducting research in an NAAB- or CACB-accredited professional degree programme, you can earn a maximum of 245 training units in training category D only.
- *Training setting 7*: If you are performing professional and/or community service when not in settings 1 through 6, you can earn a maximum of 10 training units in training category D, area 16 (professional and community service).[9]

---

[9]http://www.ncarb.org/idp/trainingsettings.htm

Obviously, if you are working in training setting 1, you will have the greatest flexibility in allocating your training units. If you are not employed under training setting 1, things get a little more complicated, and you should double check with NCARB as to which type of training setting your office fits and therefore how many units you are allowed to earn in that training setting. If you are working for an engineering firm or under the supervision of a non-architectural design or engineering professional, for example, you will need to change your employer and make up the remainder of training units in your new job in order to completely fulfil your IDP requirements. Again, please check with NCARB at the time this occurs, in case anything has changed.

NCARB also specifies several requirements for how long you need to work in a particular training area, which define the character of your employment (full-time or part-time). For example, in order to earn training units in training settings 1–5, you must work at least 35 hours per week for a minimum period of 10 consecutive weeks, or at least 20 hours per week for a minimum period of six consecutive months. This is very important when making your plans for summer employment or if you plan to work during the academic year. Make sure that you will be able to keep these working hours, so your experience counts towards your IDP requirements. Also, if you plan on accumulating your IDP training units before graduation, note that no experience used to obtain core or elective academic credit required for graduation in an NAAB- or CACB-accredited degree programme may be used to earn training units. That means a co-op programme that gives you academic credit at your school may not count towards IDP. For more information on training settings and a complete list of requirements see http://www.ncarb.org/idp/trainingsettings.htm.

## Core Competencies

NCARB defines core competencies (types of ability) that you need to acquire in each one of the 16 training areas. Basically, the core competencies outline more precisely what you should know about each training area once you complete your internship. NCARB defines two types of activity – *Awareness and Understanding* and *Skills and Application* – for each of its 16 IDP training areas.

### Awareness and Understanding

*Awareness and Understanding* encompass various sets of technical information, concepts and principles that you can articulate both orally and in writing. They refer to and rely on your learning from the two important manuals for architectural practice, which are basically your IDP "textbooks": *The Architect's Handbook of Professional Practice* (AHPP), New York: John Wiley and Sons, 13th edition, 2001, and *The Construction Specifications Institute Manual of Practice* (also known as the *CSI Manual of Practice*), McGraw-Hill Professional, 2nd edition, 2002. Purchasing these manuals might be very costly, so we suggest that you check if your office library has copies. They are also available in a more affordable student edition.

## Skills and Application

*Skills and Application* involve performance-oriented activities that form each core competency. Basically, here you are asked to apply what you have learned through reading, writing, or observing. Your application of skills may include more writing, but also drawing or sharing your knowledge in an active way with team workers or on site to make specific parts of your work happen. For the full list of core competencies you should refer to NCARB's web site http://www.ncarb.org/idp/idpdescrip.htm.

When you begin with your internship, make sure to familiarize yourself with those core competencies and compare them to your current skills and knowledge. Discuss them with your supervisor and mentor, and try to map out the most efficient way to acquire the core competencies. This will mostly depend on the kind of projects in which you are involved. Given the diversity of IDP training areas, the achievement of core competences might not come with the mere fulfilment of the minimum training units for a particular area. As you progress with your IDP, make sure that you regularly discuss your training with your supervisor and mentor. It is also important to talk to other interns and people who recently passed the licensing examination to get first-hand advice on some of the issues. As an intern, you might be asked to do work unrelated to the practice of architecture, ranging from brewing coffee to being a messenger. This is acceptable if it occurs occasionally, with the bulk of your time still spent within the field of architecture. However, if after a month or so, this is the only thing you are doing, you have a problem that needs to be discussed to which your supervisor and mentor. Also, if there are certain training areas to which you are not being exposed (or will not be in the near future), make sure to bring this up in your conversations with your mentor and supervisor. Ask to be considered for alternative assignments, which will result in more diverse training opportunities.

## Architectural Registration Examination (ARE)

Following successful completion of your IDP requirements, you will be eligible to apply to a state architectural board for admission to the ARE. Passing the ARE is in most states the final requirement for obtaining a licence to practice architecture. The ARE is developed by the NCARB and has been adopted for use by all state registration boards as the registration (or licensing) examination for all candidates for architectural registration. This means that it is the same for every state. The main purpose of the ARE is to evaluate your competence in protecting the public through your ability to provide architectural services in: "pre-design, site design, building design, building systems, and construction documents, and professional services as they relate to social, cultural, natural, and physical forces, and to other related external constraints".[10] The ARE also evaluates a candidate's general professional abilities, such as ability to work in a team, and with other professionals involved in the processes of design and construction. The ARE is a computer-based examination, available at a network of centres across the USA. It is important to know that the ARE, like the set of accountancy and law examinations needed for registration in those professions, is not an easy examination and few candidates pass all parts of it on the first attempt. Many schools of architecture offer classes to prepare you for the ARE, and in addition, students get together in informal study groups to share the process of preparing for the examination. If your own architecture school cannot help you, your local AIA chapter will usually tell you where the nearest classes may be, and if informal preparation groups exist.

After meeting your registration board's eligibility requirements and after paying the balance of your Council Record fees, you will need to submit a written authorization to NCARB to release your Record to a specific board in support of your application for examination or, if you are seeking recognition of your registration in another state, for registration in your chosen new state. In order to make sure you do not miss any steps in applying for the ARE, you should contact the architectural registration board in the jurisdiction where you plan to register as an architect. A list of all registration boards and their contact details is available from the NCARB web site. The registration board will inform you about specific requirements and examination fees. The fees might be substantial and it is wise to negotiate with your employer if they are able to reimburse you for the examination fees. Some employers will do it, some will not, some

---

[10]*ARE Guidelines Version 3.0* (Washington, DC: NCARB, 2004); p. 1.

will reimburse only once – and that is once you pass the examination (in case you are re-taking it, or parts of it, several times). Do not, also, necessarily expect a pay raise once you have passed the examination. Again here some employers will recognize your new status and other will not.

Resources

- NCARB's ARE guidelines: http://www.ncarb.org/forms/areguide.pdf
- AIA's ARE study guidelines: http://www.aia.org/idp/AREsources.pdf

*Reciprocity*

The term "reciprocity" means that once you become a registered architect in certain jurisdiction (state), you can apply for registration in another jurisdiction (state) by presenting the appropriate documentation that demonstrates you fulfil that state's requirements for reciprocal registration. You can obtain more information about reciprocity from your State Board. Like the regular registration process, you start by reviewing your academic and professional credentials. If you are registered, but only have a pre-professional degree in architecture, you may not be eligible for reciprocity in certain US states. Also, you must check if and when your intended jurisdiction has adopted the IDP training requirements for initial registration. If you were initially registered after the IDP adoption date, you will be asked to document your professional experience against the IDP training requirements, whereas if you were initially registered before the IDP adoption date you will need to seek advice as to how to record your experience. As always, there might be some exceptions to the rule, so make sure you check with your jurisdiction carefully before embarking on any additional work or paperwork for your reciprocal registration.

The good news is that between the USA and Canada there are few boundaries when it comes to practising architecture. NCARB and CCAC have signed an agreement, providing reciprocity for architectural registration in a jurisdiction that has accepted a "Letter of Undertaking." This letter provides:

> for the acceptance of the conditions of the NCARB/CCAC Agreement
> and also permits the jurisdiction/province to stipulate any special
> requirements, such as demonstration of knowledge of local laws,
> seismic forces, personal interview, or other unique requirements that
> all applicants for registration must meet.[11]

---

[11] http://www.ncarb.org/reciprocity/interrecognition.html

*Foreign Applicants*

Although the globalization of architectural markets brought significant opportunities for US architects to be engaged in practice abroad, and vice versa, there is still no reciprocal registration between foreign countries and the USA (with the exception of Canada, as outlined in the paragraph above). To become a registered architect in a certain US jurisdiction, you must fully comply with that jurisdiction's education, training, and examination requirements. If you have significant foreign experience at a high level (5 years or more in many cases, of acting as a principal of a practice) you should contact NCARB as this may be considered.

Although the registration process for architects with foreign credentials might look tedious at first sight, it is important to remember that architects are still in a much better position than some other foreign professionals (physicians or other medical professionals) for whom reciprocal recognition is much more difficult. The RIBA and the AIA have a reciprocity agreement, although this does not impact licensing/registration, it is helpful for many other support functions a UK architect in the USA might need. It is also important to bear in mind that you can still start working in an architectural office in the USA even though you have not yet became a registered architect in the USA. However, you cannot call yourself an architect, or fully embark on all the complexities of architectural profession until to you are a registered architect. Your salary and advancement within a firm might suffer too. The best place to start is to contact your State Board (their list and contact details are available on the NCARB web site) and start the process based on their instructions.

Regarding recognition of your education, educational requirements were outlined earlier on in this chapter. In seeking credit for these, you will most probably be directed to have your credentials evaluated through NAAB's EESA, which might require some additional coursework on your part to fully match your education with the NCARB requirements. Some schools offer evening classes, so you might still be able to work in an office and finish your training to comply with NAAB's recommendations. A lot of foreign nationals are surprised to find out that they might need to take courses that are not strictly architectural, such as natural sciences or humanities, for example. Depending on the architectural curriculum that you took, you may also need to take courses in professional practice that are more closely related to practising architecture in the USA. To receive the application package for evaluation of your foreign credentials and to learn more about the fees, visit the NAAB web site at www.naab.org.

Regarding recognition of your training, the requirements will basically be the same as IDP requirements, adopted by most NCARB member registration boards. Remember that a portion of your foreign training can be applied towards the fulfilment of IDP requirements. The maximum credit allowed for foreign experience in architecture is 235 training units, if you worked under the supervision of an architect registered in that foreign country (which is outlined as a training setting three earlier in this chapter).

## NCARB Certification

Once you pass the ARE and become registered to practice architecture in your jurisdiction, you are eligible to receive the National Council of Architectural Registration Boards Certificate (the "NCARB Certificate"). This is given to architects who meet highest standards of architectural education and practice. NCARB-certified architects automatically qualify for reciprocal registration in many US states and in an increasingly large number of foreign countries.

## Continuing Education

The AIA web site provides a list of states that require Mandatory Continuing Education (MCE) for maintaining licensure. It also provides options for earning MCE credits with a searchable database of courses offered by Registered Providers, along with their contact information. The National AIA web site hosts the AIA *eClassroom* (http://eclassroom. aia.org). The AIA *eClassroom* is a distance education programme that provides continuing education opportunities 24 hours a day, 7 days a week. Courses feature the most popular sessions from recent AIA National conventions, as well as seminars, ranging from design and presentation skills, to strategic business planning, and other topics.

## A Final Note

Remember that, more than anything else, internship is about you and about the advancement of your skills and intellectual potentials. In this process, you are not alone, so remember to seek advice from your peers, supervisors, mentors, faculty members, and colleagues. Together with your academic training, internship is a "practical" gateway to one of the most exciting professions – architecture. Good luck!

# 7   International Experience

In this chapter we will discuss some of the opportunities for practical experience in countries outside the UK and the USA. We will touch on a few of the many different ways of becoming an architect abroad. We will also look at some of the differences in expectations for practical experience across the world, how these, in some cases, relate to getting licensed abroad, and how to consider the spatial and cultural environment as much a part of the experience as the job itself. Finally, we will discuss on some practical issues related to working abroad like where to look for work, how to deal with visa procedures, and how to prepare yourself for life in another culture.

## Becoming an Architect Abroad

The process of becoming an architect varies significantly across the world. Some countries have very structured processes that balance professional knowledge gained through education with professional knowledge gained through practical experience. Other countries require little post-graduation experience for registration or licensure as an architect. These differences mean that an international architectural licence is definitely a far off concept, despite the fact that architectural practice is becoming more global every day. In the European Union (EU), which has passed legislation to ensure that each member country in principle recognizes the qualifications of other EU members, progress towards true mobility, and reciprocal recognition of qualifications is very slow indeed.

As one example of similarities and differences in professional registration, the process of getting licensed in Germany resembles both the UK and the US systems, but also has some differences. The first requirement for getting licensed in Germany is graduation from an architecture programme approved by the Architektenkammer (chamber of architects of each county/Bundesland), whether it is at a university, or a technical or art institution of higher education (architecture is taught at all three). Foreign degrees can also be individually approved by the Chamber of Architects. However, to become an architect in Germany as a foreign person, you would need to be a resident, so as a non-EU citizen, you would also need a work or permanent visa. Regulations are under way to automatically approve all European degrees together with introducing a university system based on bachelor and master degrees like those of the UK and the USA, but until now non-EU graduates have needed individual approval, normally granted if the graduation is a masters degree/diploma from an approved university.

The second requirement in Germany is to have documented practical experience in an office for at least 2 years (this requirement can vary slightly in different counties). During this time one has to go through all stages of the architectural work phases, from concept design, via building permit, detailed construction drawings to costing, and site supervision. It does not necessarily need to be on the same project, nor in the same office.

After meeting these requirements the candidate can register as an architect with the Chamber of Architects of the appropriate federal state. There are two possible ways of registering: as an employee, or as a self-employed architect. The registration comes with an annual fee. Both kinds of architect become a member of the "Versorgungswerk", a pension fund that also includes insurance against becoming disabled, into which each architect pays some income. The Bund Deutscher Architekten (BDA) is an association of architects for only a minority of registered architects. To become a member you have to be self-employed, have to have contributed to the culture of architecture, be member of a chamber and be nominated by the association. It is therefore a privilege and an honour to belong to the BDA. Germany thus has a two-tier system of architectural organizations, like the UK, but unlike the UK the second, more prestigious layer, requires special recognition. The BDA is more like the College of Fellows of the American Institute of Architects, made of an élite of its members. The process of becoming an architect in Germany shows that while architectural professions have similar structures in different countries, none are exactly the same.

Resource

• Bauwelt/DBZ/ARCH+: www.baunetz.de

A different way to get licensed exists in Spain, where students work at the same time as attending architectural education, spending half-a-day at work and half-a-day at school. As soon as a student finishes her final examinations at a Spanish school of architecture, she/he goes directly to their regional Colegio de Arquitectos to register as an architect. She/he only needs to pay a fixed annual fee (which covers administrative costs, library services, exhibitions, etc.) to the Colegio to register. When an architect has designed a project – before presenting it at the Town Hall – it has to be approved by the Colegio of the region where the project is going to be built. This is compulsory, and from this relationship derives the power of the Colegio – in a sense the Colegio licenses both the architect and each individual project. In case an architect is not registered in that region, her home Colegio writes an introductory letter to the Colegio of the project, allowing that architect to work in the region. Once the project is approved by the Colegio (if it follows planning regulations, regulations for disabled access, structure, building and fire regulations, environmental, acoustic and energy laws, as well as comprising the minimum number of drawings that define the project, and the architect has the appropriate insurance, etc.), the architect has to pay a percentage of her fee for this checking process. The checking fee depends on the total cost of the building. In this way, Colegios monitor both the registration process of an architect and the construction quality (if not always the architectural quality) of the building.

**Working Abroad**

It is important to be realistic when you consider working abroad, understanding that professional life in another country may be very different to experiences you have had so far. You should expect to make all of the changes necessary to adapt to your new situation, and should also remember that, however exciting it might seem, moving to another country can involve surprises, including culture shock, that you may not have anticipated. However, if you are open-minded, flexible, and patient with yourself and your new situation, professional experience gained abroad can be one of the most meaningful experiences you will ever have.

## Long Term

If you want to make a long-term move, learning about the process of becoming a registered architect in your chosen country becomes critical and you will need to do much research. You will need to contact the professional architectural organizations in that country and learn not only about requirements for professional experience but also for educational qualifications. The differences in educational and registration processes in different countries is so great in some cases, that it may mean beginning all over again, or accepting that you will not be a registered architect there. If that is the case, find out whether that means you have to always work for someone else – in some countries there is no protection of the title or practice of architect, which means anyone can design a building. In other countries, like the UK, the title of architect is protected, but the practice of architecture is not. In the UK, therefore, if you are not registered with the Architects' Registration Board (ARB), you cannot call yourself an architect, but as the practice of architecture is not protected by law, you can design buildings, as long as you do not call yourself an architect. In the USA both the title of architect and the practice of architecture are protected by law, so the only projects you can design in most states if you are not licensed (as we have said earlier each state has its licensing laws) are single-family dwellings and small apartment buildings.

If you are considering your professional experience abroad to lead to a permanent move, you will also need to consider your ability to commit to the decades that it takes to build up networks of clients, developers, community leaders, consultants, political contacts, contractors, and suppliers that underpin the activities of any successful architectural office. Architectural practice, despite the many changes associated with globalization, is still very much a site-specific activity. It relies on established relationships, whether these are local to the place in which the practice is located, or relate to a network of professionals who are highly skilled in forms of global practice, or both.

## Short Term

If you intend to spend a shorter time abroad, you will still need to prepare carefully for the transition. It is always helpful to have had prior living experience of a particular country. Language skills are also very important, even if most people speak English. You will find yourself excluded from certain conversations, both private and professional, if you are not willing to learn the language of your new home. Methods of producing buildings also vary enormously in different parts of the world. Building products and construction legislation differ. Construction methods differ, with some countries like the USA relying heavily on mass-produced industrial products and other countries relying on individual craft production. Even in English speaking countries the words for different parts of the building may not be the same, so you may have to learn a whole new vocabulary. In addition, what may seem to be totally logical to you may not fit within the logic of the constructional culture you have joined. In addition to a professional mentor, it is also very helpful if you can find a personal mentor that can act not only as your guide to the new culture, but can introduce you to a circle of friends, that can be very helpful indeed in making experience abroad a real success.

Learning about cultural traditions is also important. There are very different work patterns in different parts of the world. In parts of Italy and Spain the siesta still punctuates the working day. In many European countries you will find that vacations and lunch hours may be longer than in the USA. Whilst it is very much a part of the culture of architecture to work long hours, particularly near deadlines, in many countries personal life, and family life, takes greater priority. Being a part of these very different attitudes towards work, society and family is one of the great pleasures of working abroad.

### Finding Work Abroad

If you have decided you wish to work abroad, the first thing you need to do is find a job. Many students find work through personal connections, particularly, as schools of architecture become more international, through fellow students. Your professors will also most likely have international connections, so do not be afraid to ask them for a recommendation. Many architecture schools run summer programmes abroad, or organize field trips with visits to professional offices and organizations. Other schools will be happy to give you course credits for a summer programme abroad run by another school. All these avenues can provide helpful first contacts or, in the case of the longer summer programmes, exchanges of a semester or a year can build a strong base for subsequent professional experience. Some architecture schools also actively help find international employment for their architecture students. If international experience is of interest to you, then ask at the time of application to a new programme whether international programmes or job placements are standard policy.

A very easy route may be available to you if you are already working for a firm with overseas offices or consultants, as you may be able to follow-up opportunities for working abroad without changing your employer, and may find excellent support for getting visas and/or work permits, accommodation and health care that way.

Architectural positions are also advertised in professional magazines, though by the time these reach your school library, the positions may well be filled. If there is an online version of a professional architectural magazine, you may be able to access advertisements that way. You can also try to approach prospective international employers at conferences. Another method involves approaching an architect that has come to lecture at your school or professional organization. In this latter case you may need to be persistent, and will need to have a good portfolio, to stand out from the crowd. You may have to try more than once, follow-up the personal contact with a letter, and portfolio, and probably follow-up calls as well. It is possible that an office may think your persistence is too intrusive, so sensitivity to the individual situation of the office coupled with polite persistence, and an ability to handle rejection, are just as essential in seeking foreign work as local work.

Most importantly, you should make contact with the professional organization of the country where you intend to work. The International Association for the Exchange of Students for Technical Experience (IAESTE, http://www.iaeste.org/) can be extremely helpful in providing paid, technical work experience abroad through its members, as well as a support network ensuring a safe experience, and help with practical arrangements, such as work permits or visas, accommodation, and travel. A list of countries whose students are supported by IAESTE can be found at http://www.iaeste.org/network/index.html. The Commonwealth Association of Architects (http://www.comarchitect.org/) may have useful contacts in some countries. At the back of this book is a list of web sites of further professional architectural organizations that may be helpful to you.

If you do not have fellow students and professors, or an architecture school or office, or a professional organization that can help you in this way, you can also try family members, and mentors. If you belong to a church, or were once a member of the scouts or guides, remember that these are international organizations whose members may have contacts abroad, including architectural contacts. Language professors can also form another useful route. Embassies and consulates can be helpful. A very effective way to find work is, of course, if you have a foreign boy- or girlfriend, who has a network of contacts in that country.

*Applying*

Once you have a list of addresses and telephone numbers, you should apply in the normal way. You might want to telephone first, to see how the office likes to receive applications. Depending on their guidance, you might then send a curriculum vitae (CV), cover letter and a small portfolio of work. You should only do so if you know the office is looking for employees, as otherwise job hunting could get quite expensive. Once you have sent your materials you will most likely have to follow-up with another call to make sure they have arrived. While this is expensive, it is important as not all countries have a reliable mail service. In some cases you will have to send your work via courier, and in other cases the office will be happy to receive a digital portfolio via e-mail or reference to a web site. Always make sure you know what kind of format works for the office. In some countries Internet services, and powerful computers that handle Photoshop or AutoCAD are expensive and therefore not yet the norm.

*Interviewing*

Once your materials have arrived, you will need to agree an interview process. Some practices may be willing to interview you over the telephone, while others will give you a chance based on personal recommendations alone. Flexibility may well be related to your potential immigration status – an office that has to be responsible for your immigration processes will obviously only make an offer if you are particularly attractive and bring special skills. Be prepared for all options. Many students also apply for positions abroad while travelling on holiday, and call on offices with their interview materials on the off chance that there will be work. This is a good way to do it, because many offices like to make a character judgement of the applicant, and that can really only be done in person.

*Salaries*

Once you have gained the attention of a particular office, and negotiations are underway, it is important that you ask as many questions as possible about the practicalities of the position. You will need to find out how much the position pays. In some countries it is not unusual for student architects to be paid very little or not at all. A few countries (e.g. Sweden) list average salaries on the web site of their professional architectural organizations, so it helps to check as much information in advance, before you actually receive a job offer. If you do decide to accept a low-pay or unpaid position, remember that you are not only compromising yourself, but also condoning practices that will make it harder for the next student to negotiate a respectable salary.

### Visas

You will need to learn about visa policies, the likelihood of and time line for getting a visa, and whether your potential future employer needs to be willing to sponsor your visa application if one is necessary. In the USA, for example, attorneys can charge significant fees to handle your visa application, and some offices, particularly the smaller ones, may not be able to pay this. You will need to know whether you or the office will cover such costs before you accept the position, as the cost can sometimes run to a thousand dollars. You will also need to know how long your visa application may take as this will affect your start date. Since 9/11 global immigration bureaucracy has increased, especially in the USA. If seeking a job in the USA, if you need a visa, ask the firm to recommend an immigration lawyer so that you can find out how much the process will cost and how long it will take. You will also need to know from your prospective office for how long it might wish to hire you, which will itself relate to the visa type you are seeking. Getting a visa can be a long and frustrating process, so be patient and polite when dealing with all the people involved in the process. Visas are also not guaranteed, as in many countries an employer is obliged to show that a native employee was not available to fill the position before it can be offered to a foreigner. Visa legislation changes all the time so be prepared to do a lot of research, and keep accurate records. Do not forget that in addition to costs for the application process, you may have costs associated with travel to embassies and consulates, and remember that, after all this, you may be turned down. It is helpful to know that if you work for a firm that has offices abroad, it may have a system in place for obtaining visas for its employees.

### Health coverage

You will also need to ask questions about health coverage. Getting sick without health coverage in a foreign country is one of the worst things that can happen to you. You need to make the right arrangements, and know how much of your salary will be needed to pay for this. In countries where health services are covered by the state (the EU) you may need to have a residency qualification before you become eligible for state health support, and therefore will need to check precisely how long a residency you need. If your home country is a member of the EU, and your prospective job is also in a member country, the arrangements on the other hand are likely to be relatively straightforward and only involve some minimal paperwork. You will need to call the health services of your home country and find out exactly what to do to be covered in the host country. You may also be able to arrange health insurance in your home country that covers you in the host country, which might need to include coverage for a flight home should you get really sick. This can get quite expensive, and may significantly diminish your earnings. Some offices, particularly the larger ones in the USA, may offer private health coverage for their employees as part of the employment contract. Ask as much as you can about this, and whether your position is eligible for this coverage, as it can be a significant perk of the position. Firms with offices abroad should, as with visas, have a well-refined system to help you find health coverage, or may provide it themselves. Whichever the situation, make sure that you know exactly who is responsible for your health coverage so that should the worst happen you are ready. Learn about recommendations about health precautions for the appropriate country. For example, in certain countries you should not drink water from the public water supply. While this is information you would research were you a tourist, as you will be resident for a much longer period, your chances of getting sick increase unless you are well-informed, sensible and disciplined. Finally, you may need inoculations for certain countries before you go, with follow-up booster shots after you arrival there. Find out what the requirements are – usually embassies and consulates provide that information.

### Accommodation

Finding suitable housing is an important part of a safe and satisfying experience abroad. The office for which you will be working may be helpful, as may accommodation agencies, and professional and personal contacts. Organizations, such as IAESTE offer help with finding somewhere to live. It is helpful if you can learn as much as you can about the differences in rental contracts in the country to which you will be travelling. In some countries rent is negotiable, and in other it is not. When dealing with agencies try to establish if there is a finder's fee, as that can amount to significant sums, sometimes a month's rental as a deposit. Having friends or colleagues at your destination who can help you navigate through the detail is very helpful.

## Culture

You should learn as much as you can about the culture of your destination, including its history, customs, food, and music. You can read, take language classes, listen to music, listen to poetry, learn about art, and study the architecture of your destination. Travel guides, and in particular *"Rough Guide"* and *"Lonely Planet"*, offer good guidance about places, health, cash, visas, etc. Seek out special magazine issues that discuss not only the architecture but also the cultural background of specific countries or subcontinents. Learn about the region, city or town in which you may work so that you understand not only how you might live but also how your professional experience may contribute to the growth and development of that environment. As Indraneel Dutta, one of our contributors has said:

> It is very important to paint a background of the city before describing the experience an intern would have. It is the city that is an integral part of the training and setting, the provider for the stage to experiment.

As further examples of where to look, recently the *Architectural Record* did an entire issue on China[1] and an issue of *Architectural Design*, called *"Off the Radar"*, highlighted work in places outside of the usual architectural hotspots.[2]

Such publications can give you an excellent idea of culture, as well as architectural practice in different global locations. In the next three chapters you will be able to read about architectural practices in the UK, the USA, and other parts of the world. These case studies, written either by practitioners or interns, should help you to get a feel for the richness and differences in international architectural practice, and give you a few more guidelines for preparing to work both locally and globally. These case studies are not exhaustive, nor necessarily geographically or typologically balanced. They should, however, give you some idea of practices ranging from traditional to unusual, and include not only UK and US situations, but also a number of architectural practices across the five continents. We begin with a small selection of UK practices in Chapter 8, follow with US practices in Chapter 9 and finally describe some other international practice in Chapter 10.

---

[1] *Architectural Record*, http://archrecord.construction.com/china/ (accessed 14 July 2004).
[2] Carter, B. and LeCuyer, A. (eds.), *Architectural Design* **73(1)**: 2003.

SECTION TWO: CASE STUDIES

# 8 UK Case Studies

The practices outlined in this chapter range from architecture to surveying firms, and span large to small, critical to corporate, and locally
based to internationally active organizations. While all of the practices
below happen to have headquarters in London, the UK also has significant regional practices, and lively regional architectural cultures.
The Royal Institute of British Architects (RIBA) directory of member
practices across the country is a helpful starting point for obtaining
contact details about further practices, and the RIBA can also provide
information about local and regional chapters that should be able to
provide additional information.

## Allford Hall Monaghan Morris

London, UK
www.ahmm.co.uk

Simon Allford, B.A. Dip. Arch., RIBA, Bartlett School of Architecture
Jonathan Hall, B.A. Dip. Arch., MSc., RIBA, Bartlett School of Architecture
Paul Monaghan, B.A. Dip. Arch., RIBA, Bartlett School of Architecture
Peter Morris, B.A. Dip. Arch., RIBA, Bartlett School of Architecture

*Allford Hall Monaghan Morris* (AHMM), is an award-winning practice
with a diverse portfolio of projects. The practice has designed a broad
range of buildings and is also involved in large-scale master planning.
Having grown from four to 50 people and with budgets varying from a
few thousand to tens of millions of pounds, *AHMM* remains committed

**Figure 8.1**
*AHMM,* Raines Dairy housing project, Stoke Newington, London, UK, 2003. Photograph by Tim Soar © Tim Soar

to the principles upon which the practice was founded. The result is a body of work that retains an underlying consistency and an ever-growing diversity. The practice's work reflects the view that architecture must be satisfying to use, beautiful to look at, cost effective to build and operate, and be informed by ideas of construction. The practice's regard for a pragmatic and clear working method results in buildings that, by extension, express function in a clear and logical way. Notable award- and competition-winning projects include Barbican Arts Centre, Walsall Bus Station, Broadgate Club, Kentish Town Health Centre, Westminster City Academy, Rumford Place, Liverpool, Work/Learn Zone – the Dome, Monsoon Building, CASPAR, Raines Dairy and Great Notley, and Jubilee Schools.

*AHMM* currently employs 11 post-Part 2 and pre-Part 3 members of staff. The practice works hard to provide an environment that is both challenging and rewarding for these employees. Responsibility is assigned according to each individual's level of experience and expertise. Both Part 2 and Part 3 members of staff have the opportunity to become involved in competition work and also as part of a team on projects. These employees have a large degree of involvement in all aspects and stages of the project, from the feasibility stage and making strategic decisions within the office through to production information and making design contributions. There is a strong emphasis within the practice on involvement and exposure to not only senior job runners and partners, but also to the consultant design team, clients, and other designers for example, graphics/furniture and artists.

## Alsop Architects

London, UK
www.alsoparchitects.com

William Alsop, AA Dip.

James Hampton, year-out student at *Alsop Architects*, writes:
*Alsop Architects* are a multi-disciplinary and international practice with roots in an art-led approach and a strong association with community and cultural projects. Possessing international satellite operations, the firm has its main base in a large London office employing architects, urban planners, three-dimensional visualization experts, animators, filmmakers, artists, and writers. As such it contrasts with other large London firms and is a synthesis of commercially driven projects together with more ambitious and innovative visioning which goes against the grain of current trends towards stylistic conformity in the UK. Further, there is an informality to the company hierarchy and a relatively youthful demographic, which benefits new arrivals to the firm.

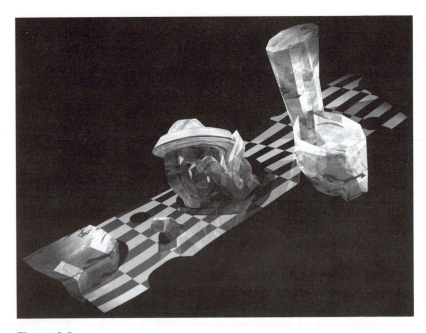

**Figure 8.2**
*Alsop Architects,* Forth Grace Project, Concept Model 2004. Digital
rendering by James Hampton for Alsop Architects. © Alsop Architects

As a year-out student at *Alsop Architects* I was given the opportunity to
be involved in a diverse range of projects from international competitions,
urban design projects to the production of construction information. The
studio environment allowed me to discover my own route, and choose
the areas of greatest interest to me. I have mainly been involved in one
project since competition stage, which I am now seeing through to submission for planning permission. Working on the Liverpool Fourth Grace
project has given me the insight and experience of seeing a project
from concept design to the beginning of its realization and I have
enjoyed being an integral part of the design process. Although my work
on this project is varied I am mainly working in three-dimensional modelling to resolve the complex geometrical issues of the design and producing presentation work for the planning submission. It should be
noted that a fairly flat hierarchy is not for everybody, as responsibility
has to be assumed for a broader range of issues and expectations
for one's contribution are very high. My own experience has been
challenging but highly rewarding and has given me the confidence and

inspiration to continue my studies with gusto. *Alsop Architects* is also the type of environment where I would seek to work upon registering as an architect.

## Arup Associates

London, UK
http://www.arupassociates.com/AA_Intro.html

*Arup Associates* integrates architecture, structural engineering, environmental engineering, cost consultancy, urban design, and product design within one studio. Every project expresses the multi-disciplinary philosophy that is at the heart of the practice. *Arup Associates'* aim is technologically advanced design that is appropriate, economic, and sensitive to environmental and human needs. The practice creates buildings and places that benefit those who use them, and that demonstrate responsibility to others who are affected by their presence. Its work is both national and international and is commissioned by clients in the public and private sectors. It undertakes projects at all scales, from urban master planning to the development of projects at all scales and components. Every project is an individual response to the opportunities presented by the client, the brief, and the site. The practice was established alongside *Ove Arup*, the engineering office, and quickly established its reputation, firstly in industrial and university buildings, and subsequently with the design of offices, concert halls, transportation facilities, and sports buildings. Its success has been found on the innovative use of building technologies and constructions processes. Its focus on the importance of building performance and the usage of land and materials has resulted in the exploration of new life for brownfield sites, and research into workplace performance. *Arup Associates* forms a focus for holistic design in *Ove Arup*. The full range of Arup's specialist knowledge and experience is available to be integrated into its project teams, to reinforce the firm's core multi-disciplinary skills.

*Arup Associates* working hours and holidays are in line with European standards. Up to two Part 1 students may be taken on each year depending on project scale and building type. Students must have genuine design talent as well as strong environmental interests. They would be moved around into different project teams to gain as much experience as possible and so they would start to form an understanding of what would be expected of them as a fully qualified architect working within *Arup Associates*.

**Figure 8.3**
*Arup Associates,* One Plantation Place, 30 Fenchurch Street, London.
Photograph by Caroline Sohie/Arup Associates. © Arup Associates

## Boyarsky Murphy Architects

London, UK
www.boyarskymurphy.com

Nicholas Boyarsky, AA Dip. B.A.(Hons), RIBA
Nicola Murphy, AA Dip.

Established in 1993, *Boyarsky Murphy* is a small, critical practice with a
reputation for experimental work. The firm is interested in form and likes

**Figure 8.4**
*Boyarsky Murphy Architects,* house addition, Eel Pie Island, London, UK.
First stage completed in 2001, second stage in 2005. Digital rendering by
Boyarsky Murphy Architects. © Boyarsky Murphy Architects

to build; it spends a great deal of energy on detailing, material research, structure, environmental concerns, and so on. Particular interests include glass and structural glazing, castings, glass fibre reinforced plastics (grp) and plastics, prefabrication, intelligent structures, and prototypes. This involves close coordination with a wide range of specialist fabricators, and consultants. To date the firm has mostly built housing projects: refurbishments, interiors, and new build houses. Examples of this work can be found in the Architecture Foundation's publication *New Architects: A Guide to Britain's Best Young Architectural Practices.*

*Boyarsky Murphy* are also interested in the social aspect of architecture and are involved in research projects, urban design, and large-scale housing projects, together with different public buildings. The firm regularly enters both invited and open international competitions. *Boyarsky Murphy* positions itself outside of the mainstream, it has no interest in commercial work. Its building projects subsidize research work and allow the practice to be independent. The office is open, friendly, and fun, a Mac environment, and busy. Everyone is involved in decision-making and the design process. The office works with models a lot; these are then refined and tested by drawing. Each project undertaken is a unique challenge and developed from first principles. The design process is exhaustive and usually involves exploring and testing a wide range of option that are then refined.

The firm regularly employs interns from all over the world including Denmark, England, Germany, North America, Israel, Spain, Hong Kong, and Taiwan. Typically they stay for 6 months or so and will be given responsibility for developing one project be it a competition, a study, a small public building, or a one-off house.

### Davis Langdon & Everest

London, UK
www.davislangdon.com

*Davis Langdon & Everest* (DLE) is an independent firm of chartered quantity surveyors, project cost, and value managers. *DLE* forms part of Davis Langdon & Seah International, operating from 86 cities throughout the UK, Europe, Middle East, Asia Pacific, Africa, Australia, and the USA. The firm has a large and diverse client base, and each year advises on construction projects with aggregate values of some £2.5 billion in the UK and £4.0 billion internationally. *DLE* manages client requirements, controls risk, manages cost, and maximizes value for money, throughout the course of construction projects. The firm also provides specialist advice and services in tax consultancy relating to construction work, specification writing, fire insurance assessment, legal support services, and industry research and analysis.

*DLE* recruits a number of year-out students every year. During their placement with *DLE* they may be involved with projects through all the development stages including feasibility, scheme design, procurement, construction, and final account. Typical tasks in which year-out students are involved include measurement of areas for estimating purposes, researching cost data, assisting with tender documentation production, visiting site, attending design team meetings, carrying out interim valuations, and measurement/valuation of variations for final account purposes.

## deRijke Marsh Morgan Architects

London, UK
www.drmm.co.uk

Alex deRijke, RIBA, ARB, M.A. (RCA) Architecture, Royal College of Art, London, Dip. Arch., Polytechnic South West
Philip Marsh, RIBA, ARB, Dip. Arch., Bartlett School of Architecture
Sadie Morgan, B.A.(Hons) Interior Design, Royal College of Art.

**Figure 8.5**
*deRijke Marsh Morgan* (dRMM), *no.one* Centaur Street Building, London, 2003. Photograph by M. Mack. © dRMM

Working at *deRijke Marsh Morgan* (dRMM) is all about (being a team player) *or* "total football", the Dutch management model strategy behind the sustained success of Ajax and the Dutch national team since the 1970s. "Total football" for *dRMM* means a collaboration whereby each team member cannot only be talented in their own area, but also must be educated in all the team positions. Roles are regularly rotated, consequently team members understand each other's ambitions and needs, communicate better, and can help each other when necessary. Personal skills are identified, respected, and developed but ideas, information, and skill transfer are more naturally and efficiently made across common experience. Each of the three partners is responsible for individual projects but every member of the *dRMM* team will directly work on all projects at particular stages. There are eight members in the team – three partners, one associate, two designers (one Part 2, one year-out student) and an office manager. The team works in an award-winning office space, part of the building that won the office five major awards in 2003 including London Building of the Year and the AJ First Building Award. *dRMM* gets many student CVs every week but can only take on one or two people a year – perhaps one year-out student and one Part 2 student. Still, the office is always interested to see what students are doing and keeps the CVs on file. When it is not working on commissioned work, it is often working on competitions and other submissions, in order to "create" new work for the future.

Panos Hadjichristofis, year-out student at *dRMM*, writes:
The gap between education and practice can seem daunting at first, especially in a big office, so I consider myself to be lucky to be part of a small team. At *dRMM*, this means that there is an informal method of learning with contributions from everyone rather than just a team leader or employment mentor. Overall, my work experience at *dRMM* has been a colourful one incorporating a healthy mixture of tasks, from animation to administration. Because this is not a big office, it is imperative to be able to contribute on different levels depending on office needs and I have been able to participate in meetings with different consultants and clients. Such opportunities would have been limited if I was working as part of a larger team with assigned position and tasks. All the three partners have had teaching experience and this was an important factor in achieving a balanced view of the profession's strengths and weaknesses. They were also able to provide me with useful advice into the inner workings of the public and private sector. The single most valuable lesson for me in my year at *dRMM* was a more thorough understanding of the process of architecture and the relationship between all the different players – architects, engineers, etc. – who help make a project a reality.

**Gollifer Langston Architects**

London, UK
www.gollifer.co.uk

Andrew Gollifer, M.A., RCA
Mark Langston, Dip. Arch., Edinburgh College of Art

**Figure 8.6**
*Gollifer Langston Architects,* Platform 1, Kings Cross, London, UK,
completed in May 2003. Photograph by James Brittain. © James Brittain

*Gollifer Langston architects* are a 12 strong practice based in Central
London, with two directors and one associate. Most of its work is
located in London, but the office enjoys the challenge of a new location.
It has tried to maintain a wide cross-section of project types but has
tended towards public, education, and arts projects in recent years.

It shares a concern that buildings and their spaces should express a sense of belonging and response to their context – giving their users a clear sense of place and location. It therefore tries to let buildings grow and resonate with the existing features of a place, while also revealing the way they work and the way they are made.

In 2004, the practice is celebrating its tenth anniversary and has about 10 projects on site, mostly between £500,000 and £5 million in construction value. The office operates with a smaller number of more highly qualified staff – the majority of the office consists of registered architects – a response to the demand of current projects. Yet the office has also seen five members of staff pass their Part 3 examination using experience in the practice during the last 4 years and those individuals have been able to see projects through completion and witness the whole process at closer hand than might be possible in a larger office.

The difficulty of recruitment in a small- to medium-sized practice is one of timing – the office can only afford to take on a new person when there is a demand, and that limits the choice to those who are available at that particular moment. Most CVs received will not coincide with such a moment, no matter how impressive. On a more positive note, though, the office is always keen to try maintaining a mix in the office of individuals from different cultures and architectural backgrounds – the practice can learn from those it employs as well as the other way around.

## Houlton Architects

London, UK

Andy Houlton, M.A., RCA, RIBA

*Houlton Architects* has evolved over a number of years by working on small projects. It has a strong commitment to making architecture that can communicate the generosity of an idea. The buildings that result from often complex design discussions are perhaps characterized by their reticence with respect to visual excess. Spatial and material use is often bold but relies upon a connection to the typology from which it has grown and reinterprets. Andrew Houlton has been associated with educational buildings and in particular "special needs" design. In 1999, he received an Royal Institute of British Architects (RIBA) Award for Riverside School for children with emotional and behavioural disorders. From this base a series of projects have been completed which combine a social commitment with aesthetic endeavour. The studio is

**Figure 8.7**
*Houlton Architects,* Beginnings Early Learning Center, West London
Synagogue, London, UK, 2003. Photograph by Paul Tyagi. © Houlton
Architects

modest in size and design commissions have remained varied, such as
health care surgeries, children's nurseries, office refurbishments, and
mixed-use "brownfield" infill sites. *Houlton Architects* envisages consoli-
dating recent work concerned with strategic urban renewal.

The office has had some varied experiences with year-out students.The quality of the experience depends upon the type of work that is passing through the studio at any given time and the temperament of the intern student. The studio is intimate in scale and whilst all project design strategies are controlled by the principal, Andrew Houlton, there is a studio culture of design dialogue. The firm has noticed that some students arrive with an expectancy to be offload without inhibition their "design ideas"; this can be disquieting to the project team who have carefully evolved a way of working and conjuring architectural responses. Other interns observe, ponder and then begin to make comments and suggestions that can gently refresh studio conversations. Students' skills upon arrival vary enormously. Many are versed in Photoshop and media graphics, some have a competent grounding in computer-aided design (CAD) drawing, understandably, few have knowledge of building procurement. Many learn and absorb new information quickly. Whilst the firm expects that interns should actively use their skills in making a positive contribution to the practice, it sees it as an "investment" to introduce students to the various "work stages" from sitting in on client briefings to visiting building sites in the company of the project architect. Some students remain in contact over the years and indeed return to work as project architects.

The practice has strong involvement, through the principal in teaching at various architecture schools in London. We believe that in the college environment students are to be encouraged to liberally discover methods of working which may define their design sensibilities. However, the studio of *Houlton Architects* expects that whilst working here students should have an attitude that is consensual, involving sensitivity for working within the present design methodologies of the practice.

# 9   US Case Studies

The firms outlined in this chapter include architectural, digital, teaching and art practice. As with UK case studies, they range from large to small, critical to corporate, traditionally managed to cooperatively run, and locally based to internationally active practices. The American Institute of Architects (AIA) will be the most helpful source of information for contact details relating to additional practices, as well as local and regional chapters where personal contacts may lead to more specific information about a particular practice.

## Garofalo Architects

Chicago, IL, USA
www.garofalo.a-node.net

President:
Douglas Garofalo, FAIA, M.Arch., Yale University, B.Arch., University of Notre Dame

*Garofalo Architects* is an award-winning internationally recognized practice located in Chicago. Speculation and innovation are at the core of the firm's contributions to the profession of architecture, acadaemia, and the larger community.

   *Garofalo Architects* produces architectural work through buildings, projects, research and teaching. With projects that vary in scale and location, the firm has actively pursued architectural design to include forms of

**Figure 9.1**
*Garofalo Architects*, "Between the Museum and the City", site-specific installation at the Museum of Contemporary Art, Chicago, USA, 2003. Photograph by Garofalo Architects. © Garofalo Architects

**Figure 9.2**
*Garofalo Architects*, study sketch for the new Center for the Visual Arts, Western Michigan University, USA, 2004. Digital rendering by Garofalo Architects. © Garofalo Architects

collaboration that cross both geographic boundaries and professional disciplines, extending conventional design practice by taking full advantage of the capacity of electronic media. The office employs animation programs from initial concept sketches all the way through construction. Western Michigan University has just named *Garofalo Architects* for its new facility for the visual arts. The firm is currently working on the new Hyde Park Art Center, and with the Mills Corporation for the development of the notorious Block 37 in Chicago. The firm fabricated two temporary structures for the Museum of Contemporary Art in Chicago, including a full-scale prototype newsstand which later travelled to Yale University. *Garofalo Architects* was a collaborator on the award-winning Korean Presbyterian Church of New York, a project that gained international notoriety as the first building truly conceived and executed with digital media, and because it represents an alternative solution to adaptive reuse.

In 2003, Chicago's Museum of Contemporary Art commissioned *Garofalo Architects* to design a temporary installation on the stepped plaza in front of museum that provided pedestrians with an outdoor public lounge. The final design emerged after an unusually diverse group of people had participated in small sessions and public forums. Cultural theorists, museum workers, educators, urban planners, engineers, city officials, college and high school students, artists, and sponsors all contributed to the design, execution, and documentation. In Pittsburgh, the firm re-configured this structure into an *animated public spatial system* (APSS) for the Carnegie Museum of Art. Presented alongside these artifacts was a video project titled *Storm Hangar*, a collaboration between Douglas Garofalo and Chicago-based artist and 1999 MacArthur Foundation Fellow Iñigo Manglano-Ovalle.

In 1995 Garofalo won the American Institute of Architects (AIA) Chicago Young Architect Award, and in 1991 was the recipient of a Young Architect Award given by The Architectural League of New York based on the theme of "Practice". In 2001 Garofalo was selected for the "Emerging Voices" program at the Architectural League of New York, was featured as "The New Vanguard" for Architectural Record, and had speculative work included in the "Folds, Blobs, and Boxes" exhibit at the Carnegie Museum.

## Herbert Lewis Kruse Blunck Architecture

Des Moines, Iowa, USA
www.hlkb.com

Founding Principals:
Charles Herbert, FAIA, M.Arch., Rice University
Calvin Lewis, FAIA, B.Arch., Iowa State University
Rod Kruse, FAIA, B.Arch., Iowa State University
Kirk Blunck, FAIA, M.Arch., Massachusetts Institute of Technology

> Iowa is the gridded center of the United States in most Americans'
> minds. What could be more American than Iowa? In my mind
> "American Gothic" by Grant Wood rises as a compelling image of the
> power of Iowa to create a heroic form from the ordinary.
>
> Tom Beeby[1]

*Herbert Lewis Kruse Blunck (HLKB) Architecture* is an architectural
practice based in Des Moines, Iowa. The practice has won more than
200 awards for excellence in master planning and architectural, urban,
and interior design. Its projects are sited from Iowa to California and
New York, ranging from a $2000 children's play space to a $25 million
corporate office complex. *HLKB Architecture* has received national AIA
Honor Awards for five diverse projects: a historical restoration, a factory,
an advertising agency, a retail store, and a complex urban project weav-
ing together a parking garage, public transit facility, and a day-care centre. In 2001, the firm was awarded the Architecture Firm Award – the
AIA' highest honor for design practice.

   *HLKB Architecture* has an inclusive design philosophy, which views
each project, regardless of scale, as a unique design opportunity. For
*HLKB Architecture*, the *idea*, the *materials*, and the *process* all coalesce
into a singular quest for *elegance*. The concept of *elegance* encapsu-
lates the difficult balance between art and science that has long been at
the root of architecture. It is precisely this balance that sets the discipline apart from other design endeavours. Of equal importance in the
development of design works is the collaborative process by which they
are completed – the elaboration, clarification, and refinement of an idea
accomplished through a studio environment that encourages critical dis-
cussion and exploration of alternatives.

---

[1]Tom Beeby, "Preface", *Herbert Lewis Kruse Blunck: Form and Technology*, Introduction
by Filippo Beltrami Gadola (Milan: L'Arca Edizioni, 2001) p. 5

**Figure 9.3**
*HLKB Architecture*, Athletic Office and Training Facility, Iowa State University, Ames, Iowa, USA, 1996. Photograph by Cameron Campbell, AIA. © Cameron Campbell

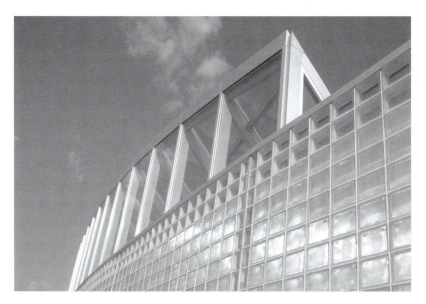

**Figure 9.4**
*HLKB Architecture*, Athletic Office and Training Facility, Iowa State University, Ames, Iowa, USA, 1996. North façade. Photograph by Cameron Campbell, AIA. © Cameron Campbell

An architectural intern employed with *HLKB Architecture* can expect a comprehensive exposure to the practice of architecture, including landscape architecture, planning, and interior design. The firm is a community of about 50 employees, including 18 intern architects and seven summer interns. The firm's commitment to a teaching-studio model emphasizes lifetime learning and mentoring, remaining the backbone of its design endeavours.

## Mark Robbins

Syracuse, NY, USA

Mark Robbins, M.Arch., Syracuse University

**Figure 9.5**
*Mark Robbins*, Empire, David (47), New York (detail), part of *Households: The Way We Live Now.* Photographs by Mark Robbins. © Mark Robbins

The work of *Mark Robbins* bridges the fields of art and architecture, encompassing photography, installations, and site-specific pieces. These projects have been celebrated for their exploration of the complex social and political forces that contribute to the built environment. In particular, his work focuses on the role played by gender and class in the construction of identity and meaning in the built environment. It relates to research and policy that has emerged in the social sciences, gender and queer studies, as well as psychoanalysis, urban studies, and economics in the past three decades. Robbins' studies of desire in the symbolic and real processes shaping urban development and architecture is seen by many in the younger generation of US architects as an important critical practice. It draws on new techniques, using multiple media to create designs and commentaries on design. More importantly, it reveals, questions, and expands the limits of current definitions of architecture by using other perspectives through which to understand the production, transmission, and consumption of architectural space and images.

*Mark Robbins'* work has been recognized through numerous awards, exhibitions, publications, and inclusion in permanent collections in the USA and abroad. In 2002–2003, Robbins was a Fellow in the visual arts at the Radcliffe Institute for Advanced Study at Harvard University where he began the *Households* project, a series of photographic portraits relating domestic interiors with their inhabitants. This work is continuing in The Netherlands, on Dutch social reform housing, as well as in Los Angeles. Among his other awards is the Rome Prize from the American Academy in Rome. After a stint as the Director of Design at the National Endowment for the Arts he is taking up the position of Dean of the Syracuse University School of Architecture in Fall 2004.

The work of the practice entails both formal and historic research about a site and its uses. It is also often involved with various techniques of production from constructed work requiring working drawings to photographic and mural installations. An attention to craft and broad intellectual frameworks are both involved. The work explores how the built environment and cultural practice intersect, and draws on earlier training in architecture. Site-specific installations and photographic work focus on the relationship between mythologies about place and information about daily life that is left out of commercial and mainstream political representations. In photographic works, such as *Households*, the concern was with the meticulous care for the body and décor, and about aging and the passing of a generation and with it, its social rituals. *Import/Export*, a series of billboards along the Miami River paired photos of maritime workers with images from tourist brochures. Earlier installation projects, such as *Telltale* in Adelaide Australia, and *Scoring the Park*, looked at the simultaneity of cruising and public space. *Borrowed Landscape*, in Saitama Japan, and *Framing American Cities* focused on the relationship between urban form and ideology in a sequence of gallery rooms. Architecture and space are used as a base for a critical practice.

**O'Donnell Wicklund Pigozzi and Peterson Architects Inc.**

Chicago, IL, USA
www.owpp.com

President:
John Syvertsen, FAIA, B.A. Georgetown University,
M.Arch. Princeton University

**Figure 9.6**
*O'Donnell, Wicklund, Pigozzi and Peterson*, Argonne National Laboratories, Aurora, USA. Digital rendering by OWP&P Architects Inc. © OWP&P Architects Inc.

> Architecture is an inclusive art that addresses the need of clients, broadly in term of services and disciplines, and deeply in term of meaning and significance.
>
> John Syvertsen

*O'Donnell Wicklund Pigozzi and Peterson Architects Inc.* (*OWP&P*) is an award-winning practice based in Chicago. *OWP&P* has a strong commitment to staff development through formal training, on-the-job coaching, and firm-supported career development mentorship between mentors and protégées at every level. While organized around the markets with leadership by focused experts, interns, and licensed professionals at early stages of their careers are not expected to commit to a specialization. Rather, they are encouraged to taste the environment, the roles and the relationships to which they become most attracted. OWP&P is award winning in every market it serves and for every discipline it provides. Many have been earned since 2000. Northside Preparatory High School, an AIA Chicago Distinguished Building and Interiors Awards recipient is on the City of Chicago's Great Chicago Places tour. A wellness centre at a community hospital received AIA Chicago, AIA/Modern Health care and Athletic Business Awards. A power plant at Banner Good Samaritan hospital in Phoenix received excellence in engineering awards from Illinois and Phoenix chapters of ASHRAE and from the American Society of Hospital Engineers. A library in Wauconda, Illinois received AIA Chicago and National Woodworking Awards and its children's library space was exhibited at the Art Institute of Chicago. An advanced research lab at the University of Chicago won an award from ASHRAE. Corporate facilities for US Gypsum received an AIA Chicago Interiors Award and finally, a land development master plan for a Native American community in Arizona was the winner of the Urban Master Planning Category of an international award program of Architectural Review.

The firm's Sustainable Design Initiative is just one example of how the firm's vision came to be embraced throughout the organization. An internal staff committee of design professionals assumed responsibility for the comprehensive education of the staff. In 2002 it established a Sustainable Design Award competition that increased in 2003 to a "Green Week" where each day the entire staff was immersed in case studies, product presentations, outstanding relevant speakers, and even movies related to the importance, techniques, client challenges, and theories of sustainable design. For this activity, the firm received recognition from Building, Design and Construction as one of the 57 Great Ideas of 2003. OWP&P has consulting and advisory roles in Chicago and with the US Green Building Council (USGBC) in establishing and assessing sustainable goals, methods, and standards. Young designers were finalists in a 2003 USGBC design award program and the Illinois Science Center at Argonne National Laboratories was exhibited at sustainable design conferences at Chicago's Field Museum and at the Chicago Architecture Foundation.

**Weller Architects**

Albuquerque, New Mexico, USA
www.wellerarchitects.com

President:
Louis L. Weller, FAIA

*Weller Architects* is a 51% Native American-owned architectural firm based in Albuquerque, New Mexico. Since its establishment in 1980, the firm has continually provided comprehensive planning, design, and construction administration services for projects located throughout the US. The firm has specialized in the design and construction management of health care, educational, community and commercial facility projects for private sector and government clients, including the 34 Native American tribes and Pueblos. Through the life of every project, *Weller Architects* focuses on delivering facilities that reflect client's social and cultural values, traditions, and expectations. The firm's vision statement, "Setting new standards for excellence and sensitivity in architecture," exemplifies the company's pride in providing a wide variety of sensitive design solutions for diverse clients.

Louis L. Weller, FAIA, the founder and President of *Weller Architects*, has been recognized nationally and internationally for his expertise in Native American architecture. Speaking engagements include the National Head Start Directors Association (Washington, DC, USA), the Austrian Association for Native American Studies (Austria), the Tampere Conference on North American Studies (Finland), and the US Senate Commission on Native American Housing (Washington, DC, USA).

An intern or a year-out student employed with *Weller Architects* will join a unique group of professionals that are interested in issues of cultural identity, namely in projects that bring sensitivity and respect for the American Indian cultural heritage. Together with an experience that encompasses all the complexities of building production in the USA – from schematic design to construction administration and management – the internship with *Weller Architects* provides a unique practical and learning experience for all professionals interested in the critical issues of empowerment and emancipation by means of architectural design.

**Figure 9.7**
*Weller Architects*, Sunshade over Entry to Taos-Picuris Health Center. The design is based on traditional building techniques with members the Spaniards called *vigas* and *latillas* interpreted here in blue metal. Taos Pueblo, New Mexico, Client: Taos-Picuris Pueblos/Indian Health Service/DHHS. Photograph by Michael Barley. © Michael Barley

## Wheeler Kearns Architects

A Collective Practice of Architects
Chicago, IL, USA
www.WKARCH.com

Principals:
Daniel Wheeler, FAIA, B.Arch., Rhode Island School of Design
Lawrence P. Kearns, AIA, B.Arch., University of Miami
Thomas Bader, RA, B.Arch., University of Cincinnati, M.Arch., Yale University
Mark Weber, RA, B.Sc., Southern Illinois University, M.Arch., University of Illinois at Chicago

A highly collaborative practice of 12, Chicago-based firm *Wheeler Kearns Architects* (*WKA*) is founded on the premise that finding the most appropriate solution must be done through critical debate, throughout all phases

**Figure 9.8**
*WKA*, Private Retreat, Northwest Indiana, USA, 1999. Photograph by Alan Shortall. © Alan Shortall 1999

of development. Each studio member has an equal voice in the development of the projects; the strongest ideas live. Founded in 1987, the office has developed an extensive residential and civic/non-profit portfolio that strives for clarity of design and technical innovation, and resolution. The firm's egalitarian philosophy and resultant work have been recognized both nationally and internationally. Notably, WKA received the Chicago AIA Firm Award in 1996, and the monograph *Ten Houses: Wheeler Kearns Architects* was published in 1999. Public sector work includes the Chicago Children's Museum, The Beverly Art Center, The Marwen Foundation, The Old Town School of Folk Music, and the North Avenue Beach House.

*WKA* is an office that is kept purposefully small. All 12 members repeat daily the activities of design, model making, detailing, writing contracts, meeting minutes, making coffee, putting on music. The office maintains strong ties to academia and the larger architectural community. Members are encouraged to teach, both in-house and in the university setting. The firm's internal education continues with a yearly trip

**Figure 9.9**
*WKA*, Marwen, Chicago, USA, 2000. Photograph by Steve Hall. © Hedrich Blessing

nationally or abroad for all staff members and spouses, to broaden the perspective of culture and current work. The office has on occasion elected to hire interns on a 1-year basis and during summers, where duties are to assist in any phase of activity. When the rare permanent staff opening occurs, applicants present their work and are interviewed informally by the entire office. New staff members typically assist a seasoned architect at first, "practising dance steps". The next move is to a relatively small "on your own" project, managing it from beginning to end, with mentoring from a principal. Once this experience is complete, project size and complexity increase in relationship to abilities. The firm has four current principals, who share that the ideal of the office is to have a partner at each desk.

## Xavier Vendrell Studio

Chicago, USA/Barcelona, Spain, EU

Principal:
Xavier Vendrell, E.T.S.A., Barcelona, Spain

Xavier Vendrell, Professor of architecture at the University of Illinois at Chicago School of Architecture, founded *Xavier Vendrell Studio* Chicago/ Barcelona in 1999. The studio is a collaborative practice of architecture, landscape architecture, and design.

Before moving to Chicago, Xavier Vendrell studied and practiced architecture in his native city of Barcelona. His work in Barcelona embraces a range of scales and practices from landscape architecture, urban design, public and private buildings, to housing and interior design. In 1988, his office won the competition for the Poblenou Park in the Olympic Village of Barcelona and was involved in several other projects for the 1992 Olympic Games. As partner of Ruisanchez-Vendrell Architects, Xavier Vendrell won the FAD Award in 1997 for the Riumar School. He has also taught at the Barcelona School of Architecture (1990–1998). He has lectured across Europe, USA and Latin America and was Visiting Professor at the Washington University School of Architecture in St. Louis, Missouri in 1994 and 1996. His works and projects have been published in books and magazines, such as *El Croquis, Quaderns, A&V, Techniques and Architecture*, and *Bauwelt*. His designes have been exhibited internationally, and in January 2002, *"Xavier Vendrell: Retrospective*

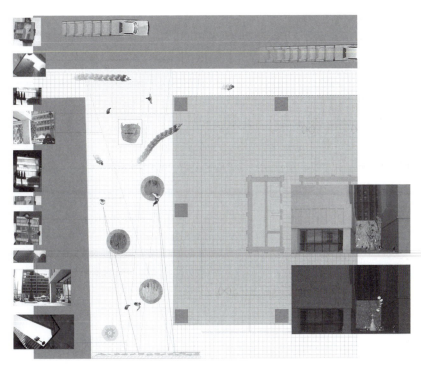

**Figure 9.10**
*Xavier Vendrell Studio*, Miró Plaza, Chicago, USA, 2003. Digital rendering by *Xavier Vendrell Studio*. © Xavier Vendrell Studio

*Thoughts on Work in Progress*" was exhibited at the Graham Foundation in Chicago.

*Xavier Vendrell Studio* sees the process of design as a synthesis of thought dealing with different issues, such as site, construction, program, users, clients, favourite movies, and other circumstances. Profoundly different for each project, these form the basis of all designs. The meaning of a project is found in the precise relationship and balance between all of these elements and ultimately, the articulation of that understanding and balance in the making of a place. The site is one of the major actors in the process of design and the creation of place. Establishing a dialogue with the site, using both harmony and tension, and drawing from the site's conditions, context, character, memory, identity, and culture, *Xavier Vendrell Studio* derives new desires and intentions. Each project is thus a response to (or a dialogue with) a particular situation in a moment in time.

An important part of the design process is the assembly of a team of qualified professionals in a variety of disciplines as collaborators in the design. An internship or a year out at *Xavier Vendrell Studio* would offer the possibility to work on projects of various scales, as well on competitions, with participation in all the phases of the architectural design process.

# 10 Other International Case Studies

In this chapter we have assembled some case studies of international architectural offices, the types of work they do, and the kind of experience a student is likely to get there. We have done so for a number of countries across the world to give you an idea of the different kinds of working environments you might encounter. It is important to remember that these case studies are neither geographically nor typologically comprehensive, and may be not typical for a particular country. Professional organizations listed in Appendix B at the back of this book should allow you to find additional information about architectural practice abroad.

## Africa

### South Africa

It has been 10 years since the advent of freedom in South Africa and the installation of a majority government. The past 10 years have seen great changes on the South African landscape with new opportunities and exciting possibilities for a young democracy. Areas of growth are primarily located within the ever-expanding tourism sector and within the public sector. The last 10 years were dedicated to developing appropriate policies and programmes for transforming South African society and learning the lessons from the various pilot projects implemented at all levels of government. The main challenge facing the government is the rate of unemployment (said to be 30–40%) and poverty with its attendant societal problems of lack of education, skills, and opportunity. In the built environment, there is urgent need to transform the apartheid landscape and to instigate development in previously depressed areas. Transforming the apartheid landscape and forging a new identity requires new and innovative approaches to architecture and urban design. This is being seen in many of the new and important state buildings (the new constitutional court, provincial seats of government, and in post-apartheid museums and cultural buildings). In order to stimulate growth, employment, and skills development the government is embarking on huge investment projects in infrastructure. Architectural practices positioned to comply with the government's procurement policies are seeing steep growth, and new and bigger challenges. Below is a selection of practices in South Africa.

## *mma Architects*

Capetown, Johannesburg, South Africa, and Berlin, Germany, EU
http://www.structural.de/text/mma-card-e.html

Mphethi Morojele, SAIA

*mma Architects* is a relatively young practice started after 1994, with offices in Capetown, Johannesburg, and Berlin, with a total staff complement of 16. Being black-owned and managed the firm's major work is in the public sector with projects being undertaken for national, provincial, and local authorities.

The office thrives on diversity in staffing and assignments, and their current portfolio ranges from prestigious government accommodation, to local community-driven projects. Recently completed projects include the South Africa embassy in Berlin, Germany, phase 1 of the Freedom Park heritage site in Pretoria and a multi-modal transport facility and market for traditional healers in Johannesburg's inner city. Current projects include a human science museum at the world heritage site "Cradle of Humankind", a children's science centre in Johannesburg and the urban upgrade of a the mixed-use city district of Braamfontein.

*mma Architects'* aim has been to establish a critical practice with a sound theoretical basis for architectural interventions within the new South Africa. They aim also to provide a platform for cultural expression of previously marginalized voices. To this end the firm has active links with the local universities through lecturing, external examinations, and engagement of students. The practice is known for its internship programme, attracting the best students from the country's four schools of architecture.

**Figure 10.1**
*mma architects*, entrance to the South Africa Embassy, Berlin, Germany,
2003. Photograph by Reinhardt Groner. © Reinhardt Groner. The design
mediates between the different public perceptions of South Africa – that
of its political past and struggle for freedom, and of its current nature and
culture-tourism appeal – and presents an image appropriate to a modern
African administration at the forefront of the global arena.

*Mashabane Rose Architects*

Houghton, South Africa
www.mashabanerose.co.za

Phil Mashabane, SAIA
Jeremy Rose

*Mashabane Rose* is the award-winning practice behind the recently completed Museum of Apartheid and the Hector Peterson Museum in Soweto, Johannesburg. Their work combines a minimalist aesthetic with a hard-hitting social agenda to produce elegant and emotionally moving public buildings. The Museum of Apartheid has been compared to Libeskind's Jewish Museum in Berlin. *Mashabane Rose* are a large practice by South African standards and after the success of their recent work, look set to become one of the country's best-known practices on the international stage.

### Ghana

Ghana was the first modern African country to win independence, in 1957. Today, almost 50 years later, the country has survived a turbulent economic and political history, and continued instability in many of the neighbouring countries has made Ghana's peaceful transition to democratic rule in the last decade even more impressive. Foreign (and domestic) investment is steadily rising. The "brain-drain" of the late 1970s and early 1980s resulted in many professionals leaving the country to study and work overseas, but, thanks in part to the political stability of the past decade, many middle-class Ghanaians are coming home. This influx has had a dramatic impact on the built environment, not least in the areas of housing and property development. As is the case with many African cities, the two major urban centres, Accra and Kumasi, are growing at an explosive rate. Lack of urban planning infrastructure and expertise has turned what were once described as "sleepy" and "garden" cities into chaotic, densely populated and rapidly expanding conurbations with all the drawbacks associated with unchecked urban sprawl. Public sector development is currently taking a back seat to private investment in both residential and commercial property. For architects and urban planners, the challenges are many and potentially very rewarding. Questions about the architectural identity of a modern, democratic West African city; the use and form of public space; the development of transport infrastructure; and the use of more culturally and ecologically sustainable materials and building techniques dominate the fledgling architectural discourse of the nation. With its outstanding heritage of iconic 1960s Modernist buildings and the powerful status of being the first country in Africa to throw off colonial rule, Ghana is well placed to emerge as a paradigm of architectural and urban development in West Africa.

## Alero Olympio Architects

Alero Olympio, RIBA

Operating out of Edinburgh and Accra, *Alero Olympio Architects* (*AOA*) is a young, dynamic practice looking at traditional building techniques and ecologically sustainable materials and researching into how these can be used in modern, urban settings. The practice works in collaboration with local masons and brick-makers have developed a low-cost, clay brick used as an alternative to the ubiquitous concrete block, found all over Ghana. Projects include the critically acclaimed Kokrobitey Institute and House Olympio in Accra.

## Ghana Infrastructure Limited

Elsie Owusu, RIBA

*Ghana Infrastructure Limited* (*GIL*) is a recently established practice run in both London and Accra in collaboration with Elsie Owusu Architects who are London based. *GIL* offer a wide range of infrastructure and architecture services, including the recently approved Rapid Transit System for Accra. *GIL* works with other consultants (transportation engineers, services engineers, etc.) to provide a full range of services and are working closely with the Ghanaian Ministry for Tourism and Modernization in urban planning and large-scale urban developments.

## Asia

### China

China has the largest population in the world, is undergoing rapid political change, and has recently had one of the fastest rates of economic growth. Population migration and urban growth pose great challenges and opportunities to Chinese architects. There are more city dwellers in China than in either the USA or Russia. Cities themselves are large and still growing: Shanghai has more than 7 million people, Beijing has more than 6 million, and Tianjin more than 5 million. Many cities have more than 1 million people each. Yet nearly four-fifths of Chinese people live in rural communities. China's cities are expanding rapidly. Urban growth is regulated to a great degree to avoid congestion, overcrowding, slum development, and unemployment. It is difficult, for example, for a person to move to a city unless he or she has a permanent job and a housing permit. Control of internal migration supports urban and regional growth patterns Chinese planners believe to be appropriate for the nation. Urbanization and migration are set to continue as China modernizes and its economy continues to grow, and this in turn provides opportunities in the built environment that have been embraced both by Chinese and foreign firms. Chinese education is also changing, with graduates successfully gaining entry into education and practice abroad, and returning home with new, globally connected knowledge. Due to restrictions on mobility, it is currently difficult (but not impossible) for foreign nationals to obtain work and residential permits. Foreign interns with experience of working in China have mostly gained this by working for a foreign practice that has partnered with a Chinese firm.

*LineSpace Architectural Planning & Consulting Co. Ltd.*

Shanghai, China

Yongjie Cai, dipl.ing/Ph.D., University of Dortmund
Zhenyu Li, M.A./Ph.D., Tongji University, Shanghai
Zhijun Wang, B.A., Tongji University, Shanghai

This Shanghai-based firm belongs to a new, young generation of Chinese architectural offices. LineSpace is driven by a strong commitment to contribute to the thriving atmosphere of economic and social growth in China today and its 10 employees have already realized a large body of commissions. The three partners met during their studies at Tongji University, one of the leading architectural schools in the country, and then worked and/or studied for a time in Germany. All have or are preparing to take doctoral degrees, and Cai and Li are Associate Professors at Tongji University. The firm's projects vary in size and include the Jimo Hotel, Conference and Exhibition Centre, and the Xinmin office building in Shanghai. A major part of the firm's work consists of high-density housing and urban developments, such as housing in the expanding city of Fuzhou. The size of the projects is scaled down in its spatial composition, showing the influence of the partners' study of the European city. This is combined with a thorough knowledge of Chinese architectural tradition and detailing, which includes consideration of the special

**Figure 10.2**
*LineSpace*, College Sichuan-1, Urban Design Competition for a
"University City" in Sichuan, 2002 (unbuilt). © LineSpace. A pedestrian
and bicycle-friendly proposal, total 3,000,000 sq m, with adminstrative and
educational buildings at the centre, surrounded by student and faculty
housing organized as a series of courtyards

status of the garden, and the use of symbolic elements, leading to a juxta-
position geometry and landscape, as in the Taihe vacation village at
Qingdao. The office is skilled in various presentation techniques, using
photo-realist animations in combination with conceptual drawings to
demonstrate the function of urban spaces, and a playful use of form and
architectural elements.

Gaining internship or year-out experience in China is not yet easy,
but offices, such as LineSpace with a broad range of work and international experience may in the future be among those that offer the best
opportunities.

### India

India has the fastest-growing population in the world, an expanding economy, and is set to overcome China in size in the next few decades. The

government has, since India gained independence from Britain in 1947, invested heavily in India's architecture and infrastructure. Urban growth has been rapid and uneven, creating particular challenges for architects, engineers, and urban planners. For a year-out student or intern the Indian immigration process is not as restrictive as China's, and foreign students have been able to get work permits and gain good professional experience in Indian architectural offices.

Resources

- Indian Institute of Architects: www.iia-india.org
- Bangalore urban projects: www.hybridarch.com/posturb.htm
- Directory of selected Indian architects: http://www.indiabuildinginfo.com/includes/consdisplaydetails.asp?menuid=98

*Zachariah Consultants*

Bangalore, India

Itty Zachariah

*Zachariah Consultants* is headed by Itty Zachariah, a fellow of the Indian Institute of Architects, and a leading figure in Bangalore architecture in the last two decades. The firm is constantly involved in projects that form the urban fabric of the Bangalore Central Business district and surroundings. The office is also part of projects that provide large-scale housing, Institutional, Software Campuses and the hospitality sector. The use of local materials and a contextual approach to a city that is famous for its British colonial era buildings is among the core design ideologies that make this firm one of the leaders in India. Mr. Zachariah is a member of the Bangalore Agenda Task Force (a body that is steering the transition of Bangalore into a global city) and governing body of the National Institute of Design. He has also held the position of the President of the Indian Institute of Architects, Bangalore Chapter.

The studio is located in the heart of the Central Bangalore D. The office has about 45 employees who, interns included, all have direct interaction with Mr. Zachariah and his senior design associates. The office has interns from all parts of India and neighbouring countries. Typically a student intern is put straight onto live projects that have short time schedules, so the experience can be intensive. Consultant interaction and attendance at client meetings are part of the experience. Making models, doing initial schemes, three-dimensional modelling and detailing are what an intern can expect to work on while at *Zachariah Consultants*. The main advantage of a firm like *Zachariah Consultants* is working on projects that are shaping urban futures. Most of these provide a wonderful opportunity to learn and be a part of a conscious effort to improve a rapidly growing city.

## Turkey

Turkey spans two continents, Europe and Asia, thus forming a bridge between east and west. A secular state since the fall of the Ottoman Empire after the First World War, Turkey's economy today is a mixture of industry and agriculture. For much of the twentieth century Turkey's economic climate has been somewhat unstable, leading to inflation and under-investment, and the migration of many Turks abroad. Internally, modernization has led to major urban growth, particularly in the capital, Ankara, and the biggest city, Istanbul. Although this has begun to blur through the emergence of suburban growth, the country's challenges can be seen both in terms of an east–west, and an urban–rural divide. Much state investment in urban and rural development, and cultural institutions, particularly in the eastern provinces, has been designed to bridge this divide. Internship in an architectural firm in Turkey may involve working on both public and private commissions, in both urban and rural settings.

### Resources

- For general information on Turkish architectural scene, a visual data base, online forums and discussions see: www.arkitera.com (soon there will be an English version available at www.arkitera.net).

### Mimarlar Tasarim – Office of Han Tumertekin

www.mimarlar.com (under construction at time of print)

Han Tumertekin, M.Arch., Istanbul Technical University

*Mimarlar Tasarim* is one of the prominent architectural practices in Turkey. Han Tumertekin is two-time recipient of National Architecture Award, and a renowned figure in Turkish architectural discourse. The office has designed and built private residences, housing, art galleries, museums, and schools, as well as office and retail projects. The office's latest work includes a bank building in Amsterdam, and a boutique in Paris. Han Tumertekin's work is well respected for simple, clean, contextual design that does not imitate its context. The size of the office is generally less than 10 people, and has been located in historic Bosphorus neighbourhoods throughout the years.

**Figure 10.3**
*Mimarlar Tasarim,* office of Han Tumertekin, B2 House – Ayvacik, Canakkale, Turkey. Photograph by Cernal Endem. © Cernal Endem

Internships are typically perceived as work in the summer months in Turkey, and they follow the minimum wage legislation. Although not an accurate reflection of Turkish architectural scene, an intern's duties at *Mimarlar Tasarim*/Han Tumertekin may include – in no particular order: surveying, model making, acting as a construction site mole, archiving, sketching, CAD drawing, and coffee making. Getting involved and acting as a design critic during the design process is just as welcomed. The office acts as one team during the initial design decisions, then each project is run by Tumertekin and a staff architect.

An architectural student at *Mimarlar Tasarim* may find that an experience closer to a studio environment in school can actually work in the real world. Since the summer internship season is short, candidates should not expect to play a major role, however the office does allow freedom to peek at and question all stages of an architectural practice. This does not mean that interns are only flâneurs; in specific instances office expects interns to act on their own judgment, as an extension of its team spirit and trust. Students should be ready for an environment where architecture is not valued on its square footage, but on the number of sketches produced until all are comfortable with the solution.

## Europe

### Czech Republic

The Czech Republic, a small Central European nation, has undergone major economic and cultural change since the "velvet revolution" of 1989. Foreign investment has been significant, and in particular the capital, Prague, has seen major private development. Public sector work has, in contrast, been limited. Many foreigners have moved to the Czech Republic, mainly to Prague, because of economic opportunities, and a relatively low-cost life style, leading to new foreign (particularly American) subcultures. Changes in the education system have also meant that most of the younger generation of Czech professionals now speaks English, and Czech architecture students have been exposed to and embrace many ideas that were out of reach 15 years ago. This has generated a group of talented young practices with an international outlook. Opportunities in such offices include retail and office space, hotels, private houses and apartments, small urban developments, and infrastructure projects.

### Resources

- Architectural organizations: www.cka.cz, www.arch.cz, www.archiweb.cz
- Zlaty Rez (Golden Section) Magazine: www.zlatyrez.cz

*Architektonická Kancelář Roman Koucký*
Prague, Czech Republic, EU
www.koucký-arch.cz

Roman Koucky, Architect, KCA

*Architektonická Kancelář Roman Koucký* is an award-winning practice
based in Prague. It is a think-tank office with a wide range of projects

**Figure 10.4**
*Architektonická Kancelář Roman Koucký,* Swan house in Sternberk,
Czech Republic. Photograph by Ester Havlová. © Ester Havlová.

**Figure 10.5**
*Architektonická Kancelář Roman Koucký*, Mariansky bridge, Czech Republic.
Photograph by Ester Havlová. © Ester Havlová.

ranging from urban proposals to interior design. At around seven to ten architects the office is quite typical in size and in range of work for a Czech architecture firm. The engineering parts of its work are subcontracted to consultants. As Roman Koucký also leads an architecture studio at the Faculty of Architecture at the Czech Technical University in Prague, the advantage for an international student working for the Koucký practice is a wide range of contacts and quick exposure to Czech architectural culture. Roman Koucký works all over the Czech Republic, and most of his projects are outside Prague.

The disadvantage of a student working for the practice is the same as with all other Czech design architectural studios – there is no or very little financial compensation for the work of students in general. The student can expect to be paid a little, and then only if his or her input into the projects is considered to be more valuable than what she/he has received in experience and extra time and energy given by other members of the office.

Resources

• Information on the work of Koucký's students at the FA CVUT: www.cbox.cz and www.cbox.cz/koucky-studenti

**France**

France, as one of the leaders of the European Union (EU) has strong public and private investment in architecture, urban development and infrastructure. It also continues to be a popular place for foreigners to seek work, not only for economic but also for cultural reasons. Architectural education places much emphasis on urban issues, and there is a growing sense of frustration felt by many French architects about the suburbanization of French cities. The legacies of colonialism, particularly in North Africa, have also made the integration/autonomy of minority populations a hotly debated issue, with important implications for urban planning and architecture.

*Rolinet et Associés Architectes et Urbanistes*

Paris, France, EU

Marc Rolinet, Architecte D.P.L.G., Urbaniste E.N.P.C.

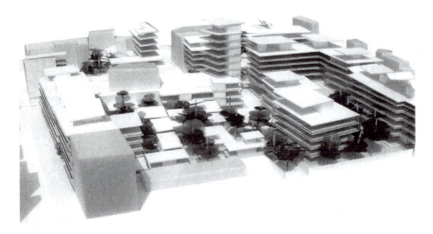

**Figure 10.6**
*Rolinet et Associés*, Site model of Ilot Chablais-Gare, France, 2003.
Photograph by Dan Shapiro. © Rolinet et Associés

*Rolinet et Associés Architectes et Urbanistes* is an architectural firm located in Paris, with a specific interest in urban design. Marc Rolinet, principal of the firm, working side by side with clients and contractors, guides the office to develop well-crafted urban design plans, integrating dense urban areas with commercial, residential, and open green spaces.

While working at *Rolinet et Associés* a student can be expected to help on competition entries, as well other work. An example of the kind of urban project in which a student may participate may include a 45,000 square metres of urban development, incorporating private residences, commercial/residential mid-rises, a Cineplex cinema, an open market, parking, and landscape design. Other projects in the office range from residential/single multi-family, commercial, and renovation/restoration projects.

Working hours in an architectural firm in Paris tend to run between 10:00 a.m. and 7:00 p.m. While one is expected to learn a great deal from both the firm's projects and its co-workers, the office space should not be confused with school life. Model making and fixing red-marks are the official trademark of the intern. A student should expect to work on small and sometimes boring jobs, but know that every job is given for a good reason. Finally, it is important to know that in many offices in France, while work is important (and expected to be completed by its deadline), work officially and mentally ends at the end of the day. Like one former co-worker once said, "we work to live not live to work".

### Germany

Germany is the other major partner in the EU. The unification of Germany has also made Germany the largest country in the EU, but came with a high cost of bridging the social and economic divide. Germany's architectural production was until recently organized around a very strong public building market ranging from schools to housing, and a strong culture of architectural competitions. This market is mostly gone. The economic differences between east and west led to some public and private investment in the east and the shortage of architects in the east created additional opportunities. Germany has a large number of small- and mid-size offices, which work in a holistic manner from concept to completion, including specification writing and the measurement of quantities, working drawings production, costing and site supervision. German architects follow a tradition of high precision in their work but face a harsh economic climate which is eroding this tradition. Specialization in the building industry is also bringing a lot of new "professionals" as service providers for architects.

Due to the speculative nature of many projects, students may find themselves doing a lot of presentation work for feasibility studies. If a student has the chance to work in an office dealing with existing buildings s/he has the best chance of gaining construction experience. There is a strong focus on environmental issues because of federal legislation, impacting the production of working drawings in particular.

Resources

- Architektenkammer (with links to all 16 individual county chambers): www.architektenkammern.de
- Bundesarchitektenkammer (the federal representation of Kammer interests): www.bundesarchitektenkammer.de
- Bund Deutscher Architekten: www.bda-architekten.de
- Baunetz: www.baunetz.de


*Sauerbruch Hutton Architects*

Berlin, Germany, EU
www.sauerbruchhutton.de

Matthias Sauerbruch, AA Dipl
Louisa Hutton, AA Dipl

Louisa Hutton and Matthias Sauerbruch founded *sauerbruch hutton architects* in 1989. Graduates of the Architectural Association in London, Matthias had previously worked for *Office of Metropolitan Architecture* (*OMA*) and Louisa had worked for Peter and Alison Smithson. After winning a major competition in 1991 – for the GSW Headquarters in newly unified Berlin – they opened a Berlin office in 1993, which is now their headquarters. The GSW Headquarters is an assemblage of four new buildings in combination with an existing tower from the 1960s. In its combination of the disparate spatial fragments of consecutive generations, this grouping puts forward the idea of conglomerate growth as a model for urban development. The new slab in particular is innovative in its use of passive – that is, architectural – means for climate control; at the same time as it offers a re-definition of environmental architecture in terms of well-being and sensuality.

   The office has since won several national and international competitions, and has completed a series of prize-winning buildings in Germany. Today Matthias Sauerbruch is Professor at the Stuttgart Art Academy, while Louisa Hutton is a Commissioner for CABE in the UK and was recently elected into the presidential council of the national Baukultur-Stiftung. The office employs some 45 architects from many countries and is distinguished by its intense professional working atmosphere and independent thought processes. Two former project architects, Juan Lucas Young and Jens Ludloff, have become junior partners.

**Figure 10.7**
*Sauerbruch Hutton Architects*, GSW Headquarters, Berlin, Germany, 1999.
Photograph by Jan Bitter. © Jan Bitter

*Passe Kälber Architekten*

Berlin, Germany, EU
www.passe-kaelber-architekten.com

Ulrike Passe, Dipl. TU Berlin
Thomas Kälber, Dipl. TU Berlin

**Figure 10.8**
*Passe Kälber Architekten, House Marxen*, Niedersachsen, Germany,
2003. Photograph by Thomas Kälber. © Passe Kälber Architekten

*Passe Kälber Architekten* was founded in 1992 by Ulrike Passe and
Thomas Kälber. The office started its career with speculative and critical statements on emerging planning debates by curating exhibitions
and producing alternative urban proposals. Both architects taught at the
Technical University of Berlin and are part-time lecturers in the University
of Kentucky Berlin programme. The firm's aim is to bring the engineer
and the artist in the profession closer together by intertwining ecological
debates on sustainability and active, passive use of solar energy with
theoretical and artistic debates on form and perception, resulting a
holistic spatial approach to sustainable detail. Building concepts use
integrative technical planning and a three-dimensional composition of
space, airflow and thermal mass for climate control, as in *House Marxen*,

designed and built for a private client near Hamburg. Durable materials, such as larch, aluminium, glass, and concrete additionally interact as membranes, moderating the external climate to formulate a well-tempered internal environment. Similar concepts are used in the design of larger-scale public and commercial building concepts. The office uses traditional and computer-aided tools and methods to mould ideas into space, construction, and material. Students interested in working for the firm should be prepared to think independently in different scales, materials and methods, and also be prepared to assist with the making of three-dimensional model by hand as well as on the computer.

## Iceland

Iceland, with a population of only 288,000 people, is the smallest and most sparsely populated nation in Europe, yet has one of the highest standards of living. Its economy centres on fish and fish products, and this, together with industrial expansion, has recently brought significant wealth to the country. The lack, until recently, of an Icelandic architecture school has meant that the current generation of Icelandic architects has been educated abroad. Such a small country does not have too many opportunities for architectural employment for foreigners, and this makes seeking work, work permits, and accommodation difficult, as mentioned below.

Resources

- Icelandic Architectural Organizations (Arkitektafélag Íslands): www.ai.is
- Arkitektadeild og hönnun, Listaháskóli Íslands: www.lhi.is

*Yrki Architects*

Reykjavik, Iceland
www.yrki.is

Ásdís Ágústsdóttir, Diploma, Bartlett, UCL
Sólveig Berg Björnsdóttir, AA Dipl.

The name *Yrki* has specific meanings in Icelandic – to cultivate and to write verse. This gives a hint of the office's philosophy, to unite the earthly and the lyrical, to show sensitivity in intertwining different inspirations for the project, from the urban to the natural, taking a coherent position

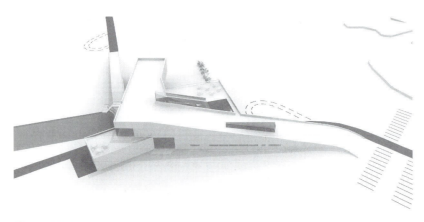

**Figure 10.9**
*Yrki Architects*, Cultural Centre in Alftanes, Iceland, 2004. Digital rendering by Arnar Gunnarsson. © Yrki Architects

**Figure 10.10**
*Yrki Architects*, Home for disabled people in Hafnarfjördur, Iceland, 2001, Photograph by Thordis Erla Águstsdottír. © Thordis Erla Águstsdottír

in relation to the designated site. *Yrki Architects* is a small architecture office in Reykjavik and has little desire to expand. It has been involved in very diverse projects and competitions, and its current portfolio of completed projects and works in progress includes a cluster of apartment blocks linked to a service centre for the elderly and a nursing home, a home for disabled people, a freezer storage for a shipping line, single-family houses, recreation homes, as well as a number of museum projects. The work of the office has been reviewed in Icelandic magazines and on state television.

Currently the staff numbers five people, Icelanders who have studied in different schools around the world because the Department of Architecture in the Arts Academy is still so young that it has not yet graduated any architects. The conversations in the office are therefore very broad and open as diverse methods, and skills are brought forward from different educational institutions. Although some architecture offices look for Icelandic speaking students, *Yrki* works both in English and Danish, and will consider applications from enthusiastic and hard-working students. However, practical matters (e.g. work permits or accommodation) may be problematic.

## Latvia

As an emerging country, Latvia is undergoing changes resulting in development at many levels, including architecture and urban planning. It preparation for membership of the EU. Latvia's has meant that it has undergone significant privatization, as well as changes in its education system. The growth in urban development and industrial investment has led to new work for architects in the retail, commercial, and cultural sectors. The re-orientation from east to west has meant that many Latvian students have taken opportunities to study and work abroad. The challenges facing Latvia, as in many Eastern European nations, comprise the growing gap between rich and poor, and emerging unofficial economies. A year-out student in Latvia should not have difficulties with visas or accommodation. However, salaries and living conditions may not be comparable to those in Western Europe and North America.

### ARHIS Ltd.

Riga, Latvia, EU
www.arhis.lv

*ARHIS* is one of the largest architecture firms in Latvia, with diverse work ranging from large-scale government buildings to small custom designed interiors, and is actively involved in most of the issues connected to urban development, including that of Riga, the capital of Latvia.

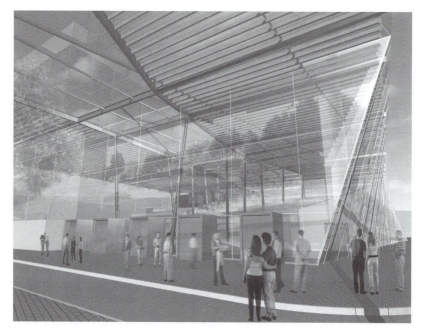

**Figure 10.11**
*ARHIS Ltd.*, "Sound of Dune", Concert Hall in Ljiepaja, Latvia, international competition entry, 2003. © ARHIS Ltd.

The *ARHIS Ltd.* was founded in 1991. The scope of its work comprises development of designs for construction, including architecture, interior design, and engineering projects. These works are often carried out in collaboration with engineering offices or with independent engineers as subcontractors. *ARHIS* manages the entire design process through such collaborations as well as through cooperation with independent architects or architecture offices. *ARHIS* also performs the supervision of the project construction phase. *ARHIS* currently employs just over 20 people consisting of architects, architecture technicians, architecture students, and managers. The majority are graduates of the Riga Polytechnic Institute or Riga Technical University, and many of them are members of the Latvian Union of Architects, with professional experience varying from 12 to 28 years working in large design offices as well as municipal authorities.

In both design and construction work various local and foreign materials and building systems are used. The designs are carried out with the help of professional computer-aided design drawing and visualization programs. Since the foundation of *ARHIS* the office has created more than 400 proposals for new construction, reconstruction, town planning as well as sketch and preliminary designs.

## Spain

Spain has experienced tremendous social and cultural change since the end of the Franco regime in 1975. The growth in its economy, both in the production and service sectors, together with strong civic leadership have resulted in major urban and regional growth, and many opportunities for architects. Cities like Barcelona have invested heavily in urban infrastructure and architecture, carefully interwoven with existing historical forms, and have thus come to stand as global models for effective urban development. The close integration of education and practice, and the locally oriented system of Colegios has supported, for the most part, the emergence of distinctive forms of neo-modernism in public buildings, which have in part tempered the expansion of low-grade commercial suburban development.

Resources

*   Spanish Architectural Organizations (Consejo Superior de los Colegios de Arquitectos de España): www.cscae.com
*   Escuela de Arquitectura, Universidad de Alicante: www.ua.es/arquitectura

*José María Torres Nadal Arquitectos*

Alicante, Spain, EU

Dr José María Torres Nadal, Ph.D., Escuela Tecnica Superior de Arquitectura, Barcelona

As Professor of Design at the Alicante School of Architecture and editor of the collection of books *Arquilecturas*, José María Torres Nadal (JMTN) has been always interested in research through buildings. Although his studio started in Murcia as a typical Spanish office of 2–3 members developing single houses through a close relationship with clients, it has grown into a regional firm with nine employees. JMTN's collaborators are young architects and students from different schools in Spain and from abroad. Both English and French are spoken in the office. Each office member is in charge of developing a project under JMTN's guidance. The office insists on the value of dialogue and encourages each member to make a contribution from his or her own experience. Projects range from single houses to invited competitions, such as the new Murcia airport or his winning proposal for a hospital in Cartagena.

**Figure 10.12**
*José María Torres Nadal Arquitectos*, Tourist Education Centre at Torrevieja, Alicante, Spain. Photograph by Juan de la Cruz Mejias. © José María Torres Nadal Arquitectos

**Figure 10.13**
*José María Torres Nadal Arquitectos*, Cartagena Regional Hospital, Murcia, Spain, 2003–present, in development design phase, digital rendering. © José María Torres Nadal Arquitectos

Bibliography

*Documentos de Arquitectura.* Issue No. 17, José María Torres Nadal. *El Croquis* No. 76

### *Sweden*

Sweden, like other Scandinavian countries, has successfully balanced a free-market economy with a strong welfare system. With most of its wealth coming from industrial production, Sweden has maintained a high standard of living for many decades, although recently this has come under pressure. Investment in communication technologies is high, spurring growth in new high-tech industries. The stable economy and strong public building programme has created a supportive climate for architects. There is much interest in sustainable design and the web site of the Swedish Association of Architects offers information to job seekers.

Resources

- Swedish Association of Architects: www.arkitekt.se
- Some main Swedish Architectural firms
  - Sandell Sandberg: www.sandellsandberg.se
  - White: www.white.se
  - Wingårdh Arkitektkontor: www.wingardhs.se
  - Smaller Swedish practices (in Swedish only): www.arkitekt.nu

*Testbedstudio*

Stockholm, Sweden, EU
www.testbedstudio.com

Dr Anders Johansson, AA Dipl London, KTH Stockholm
Fredrik Magnusson, LTH Lund
Jonas Olsson, LTH Lund

*Testbedstudio* is a small Swedish practice, oriented both towards building and urban planning. *Testbedstudio* consists of six people, and has offices in Malmö and Stockholm. The work of *Testbedstudio* is based on a strategic approach, with architecture and urban planning as components

**Figure 10.14**
*Testbedstudio*, Pavillion for Swedish Telecom in the National Building Expo Bo01, Malmö, Sweden, completed in 2001. Photograph by Jeroen Musch.
© Testbedstudio

**Figure 10.15**
*Testbedstudio*, Interior for MINC, Malmö, Sweden, completed in 2002.
Photograph by Jeroen Musch. © Testbedstudio

within the same programmatic considerations. *Testbedstudio* mixes formal design with research. It offers clients a range of complementary services, such as forms of projective analysis, coordination of dialogue and citizen participation, and involves a network of collaborators in different professional fields.

A student working with *Testbedstudio* will partake in all aspects of the project. Students are expected to be self-directed and motivated, and are given a high degree of responsibility. They have to be well versed in forms of architectural representation and modelling, as well as having writing skills. Knowledge of Swedish language is very helpful but not required. More information about architectural practice in Sweden is available on the web site of the Swedish Association of Architects.

## Latin America

### Argentina

Argentina has been an independent nation for nearly 200 years, but until 1983 had a series of tumultuous political regimes that destabilized its economic and social progress. The country's natural resources are

**Figure 10.16**
*Gerardo Caballero*, Apartment building, Rosario, Argentina, 2000.
Photograph by Gustavo Frittegotto. © Gustavo Frittegotto

extensive and its education system is strong. Both public and private sectors have acted as springboards for practices of talented Argentinean architects, although the uncertain economy makes architectural practice in Argentina a continuing challenge. Uncontrolled commercial and informal growth at urban peripheries poses further challenges, and urban issues form a large part of architectural debate both within the profession and within architectural education.

### Resources

* FADEA Federacion Argentina de Entidades de Arquitectos: www.fadea.org.ar

*Gerardo Caballero Architect*

Rosario, Argentina

Gerardo Caballero, M. Arch., Washington University, St. Louis

Gerardo Caballero established his award-winning practice in 1988 in Rosario, Argentina and has taught at the Harvard University Graduate School of Design. Currently, as a Professor at the School of Architecture at Washington University, St. Louis, he is the Director of Graduate Program Abroad in Buenos Aires, Argentina. His practice has won several national and international competitions, and his work has been published in international architectural magazines, such as *Quaderns* and 2G. With influences that include American Land Art and the work of Alvaro Siza, the work of Gerardo Caballero relies on a poetic synthesis of abstraction and sensibility, leading to a body of work in which architectural ideas are framed by precisely constructed relationships with the landscape, and where site conditions are understood in a much broader sense as cultural conditions. With a regular staff of four people, and models hanging on its white tall walls, the office of *Gerardo Caballero* is a gentle laboratory of architectural production. The doors of the office are always open, and if you glance through the window you will find him quietly drawing something on his desk. An internship experience at his office might include participating in competitions and private commissions, each developed with the same conceptual precision and architectural sensibility.

### A Final Note

These form just a few of the many different architectural working environments across the globe. Many of the office descriptions here were written by contributors who have themselves been student employees in these offices. We hope this has encouraged you to think about working in another country, and given you some idea of the differences as well as similarities in international architectural practice. In the next chapter, now that you have an idea of where you wish to work, we will outline some strategies for getting there.

SECTION THREE: HOW TO GET THERE

# 11  Finding a Job

In this chapter you will learn how and where to look for the right practical experience. We will also discuss your application package and
how to prepare for an interview.

## How Can You Find the Right Job for You?

You will need to ask yourself some questions before you look for "the
right position", whether it is in a traditional architectural office, or an office
that is more unusual. The right job will depend on a number of things –
basically on a good fit between you, the position and the practice.

First, what kind of experience are you looking for? Which kind of office
will offer the type of experience that you need or desire? In Chapter 3 we
outlined many types of practice potentially able to provide you with practical experience during your internship or year out. Whilst you may not in
the end to have too much freedom to choose, and may have to take what is
available, thinking about the ideal situation is useful if you have enough
time to prepare, and present your work and yourself as a good fit for the
office.

To be able to see whether you may be a good fit for a position you will
need to understand the job market. This means doing some extensive
research. Think carefully about what kind of work you would like to do,
where would you like to do it, and then define the most appropriate strategy to get the position. Many firms have web sites, and that is the best
place to start. Look at projects, see if you would be happy working on
them, and whether you have skills that would make you attractive to that

office. Some firms also publish annual journals, like the *Skidmore Owings and Merrill Journal* in the USA, or might have a monograph on their design work. Look for those publications in the bookstores and on the web, and see if your portfolio can complement their area of expertise. If a firm does not have a web site, call anyway, and ask them to send you their publicity brochure or practice portfolio, or copies of publications about their work. Do not dismiss a firm because it does not have good publicity materials. Some firms work with long-standing clients, and may not need publicity.

Wherever you apply, you will have to have something the office needs. At the most basic level this might be that you are cheaper to employ than more experienced job seekers. It would be better if you could also add to that your enthusiasm, flexibility, and keenness to learn. Ideally you would also be able to bring a set of skills to an office that the office currently lacks. You should aim to get as close to this ideal situation as possible.

You will therefore need to evaluate your current strengths and weaknesses, and try to find as many skills that are unique to you. Do you have construction experience helping a family member build so that you bring some understanding of the building site? Have you been involved in community activities so that you bring skills in communicating with non-architects, or diverse populations? Do you speak a language? Have you worked abroad? Do you have a high level of skill using digital media? Have you built one-to-one details in the studio? Do you have a wonderful measured drawing in your portfolio? Can you write well? If the answer to any of these is yes, make sure you document as much of this strength in your portfolio.

You do not have to evaluate your strengths and weaknesses alone. One of the best ways to evaluate yourself is to sit down with the professor who you feel has the greatest understanding of your work, or if you already have a mentor for your year out or internship year, then sit down with your portfolio and résumé, and with their support start to go through your strengths and weaknesses, one by one. You can ask more than one person to help you. Obviously, the sooner you do this the better – a full year before you are due to seek employment is ideal as it will allow you to try to improve on your strengths and eliminate some of your greatest weaknesses. You may be told that the sense of colour in your work is lousy, or that you do not have a complete enough set of drawings of your favourite school project to convince your mentor or professor, or that your understanding of computer-aided design (CAD) programs is basic at best. If you learn those shortcomings early, you should be able to do something about them before the interview season arrives. As you establish your strengths and weaknesses try to see whether they fit the position you seek.

Third, call the office or offices in which you would like to work and ask them what they would be seeking in an ideal candidate for a year out or internship. Some offices will tell you that they do not take interns or unqualified architects. Some offices may be unclear about what kind of employee they seek. Others will be precise, and may even point you to a current or former employee for further advice. You may also have a friend, or your professor or mentor who may know someone in the office. Call and find out informally what a strong candidate would need to have in terms of experience and portfolio.

There is a final crucial question. You will need to know the state of the economy of the area where you wish to seek work. If there is a regional, national, or global recession, jobs will be scarce and even strong applicants will be unable to find work in the areas they prefer. Be flexible – if there is no work in an architect's office, work for a construction company. Consider working in another country, in the Peace Corps or Voluntary Service Overseas. Management or landscape experience, a second language, or a unique cultural background may become very useful later on. If there is a really bad recession, you may wish to wait to do your internship after you have finished your diploma or masters degree.

### *Job Availability and Where to Find a Position*

For the purposes of this book we assume that you know what kind of practice you seek, you know what your strengths are, and the economy is good. To find the right job, you may wish to send a large number of application letters, but if you wish to narrow down the field, how do you find which offices are hiring? Apart from advertisements in architectural and construction magazines, there are numerous web-based resources to help you. Your school may have a web site to which its alumni and other employers post job advertisements. Your school may have a co-op or job placement programme. Local, regional, or national architectural organization may have a web site with job opportunities. Take a look at the list at the end of this book for the web sites of many professional architectural organizations across the world. Some offices will be used to enquiries, and will respond in a timely and polite way, whereas others will not. Some may be helpful, and others may not.

In the UK, the number of positions for Stage 1 "Year-Out" students, and post-Part 2 Graduates otherwise known as Architectural Assistants, vary enormously depending on where in the UK you decide to work. Over a third of UK practices are situated in London and the south-east, but inevitably this is also where the greatest competition will be for jobs.

Remember that you will be in competition not only with students who have studied in the UK, but many from Europe, the USA, South Africa, and the Far East – all looking for good experience and the opportunity to live and play for a while in London or close by.

Having an open mind about the location where you might work can be extremely beneficial, as living expenses are always far lower outside of the south-east. A useful strategy can be to look at which cities or areas of the UK are undergoing large amounts of new construction – one way you can find that out is by carefully reading UK architectural magazines. It is always advisable to identify practices whose work you admire or respect and to do plenty of homework on the current work of the firm. Of course it is helpful if your portfolio contains student projects that deal with issues closely connected to the specialization of the firm.

It can also prove useful to become a student (Stage 1) or Graduate (Stage 2) member of the Royal Institute of British Architects (RIBA). The RIBA is a focal point for UK architects and has an excellent library and members' information services that student members may use. Although anyone may use the RIBA, as a member – particularly if you are trying to network and set up contacts – you will be informed of all the activities and events, will have the opportunity to buy cheaper tickets for some events, and may be able to make important informal contacts with leading practitioners. Networking skills are useful in themselves, and also lead to opportunities, sometimes immediately, and sometimes later.

The RIBA has set up an invaluable web site, all based at www. architecture.com for general information and events and www.pedr.co.uk, which provides specific guidance on professional experience employment and studies. In particular, when looking for Stage 2 post-Part 2 Graduate Employment vacancies, you can register with RIBA Appointments via their web site at www.architecture.com and www.riba-jobs.com. This is the Recruitment Consultancy of the RIBA available to all UK resident members of the profession (i.e. not just members of the RIBA or qualified architects – any students and graduates studying towards Parts 2 and 3 can use these services). Stage 1 "Year-Out" students are no longer catered for on this site, but a new service is being developed at www.pedr.co.uk where employers will be able to advertise Stage 1 "Year-Out" vacancies. This service is available as of summer 2004. Other places where you will find year-out positions advertised include *Building Design*, the profession's weekly newspaper, *The Architects' Journal*, and other architectural journals and noticeboards in various schools of Architecture.

Although these are useful sources, there is of course nothing like having already made contact with a firm through work experience, networking, exhibiting, etc. Identifying the work of a practice that you particularly like and then writing to them with a curriculum vitae (CV) and some images of your work is another, proactive method of finding employment. You can find the contact details of any registered practice via the RIBA's Practice Directory (go to www.riba.org.uk "find an architect").

Previous part-time or summer work is an excellent means of gaining a placement. Sometimes a former employer may be willing to call a colleague on your behalf. There is no harm in asking, the worst answer (no) will leave you no worse off than not asking at all. If you are a UK student, your end of year exhibition is also important. Many larger practices approach students after they have seen their work in this context. If you are a foreign student, taking part in one of your school's Study Abroad programmes (if it has one) will allow you a great opportunity to participate in events and other professional architectural activities of that country, and get to know people who might later be able to help you to find a job.

Getting to know people and networking within the profession is always useful and many students get involved in related extra-curricular activities that can create contacts with practising professionals. One useful route is ARCHAOS, the national student architectural society, founded in 1999 by the student representatives who sit on the RIBA Council.

In the USA, the American Institute of Architects (AIA) has a web site (www.aia.org) with a link for job seekers, which is basically a search engine that helps you find various job vacancies in the USA. You can also subscribe to e-mail notifications and updates on future job openings. You may also contact local AIA chapters and ask them about current job postings. Some regional offices are very helpful and they will often fax you a list of vacancies or at least guide you to their web site where you can obtain such lists. If you are thinking of working abroad, the language barrier might be a problem. Some organizations abroad might have bilingual web sites (including sites in English), but if not, try calling them on the phone and talking to someone who speaks English and can answer your questions. The other option is to go to job fairs, organized by some universities or professional associations. These job fairs are generally open to many different fields, so you need to make sure that architecture is represented. If you decide to participate, come prepared and bring your cover letter, résumé and portfolio. Since job fairs are basically job interviews, please refer to the rest of this chapter for more information on different interview strategies.

You have done your homework. You have a list of offices, you know what you have to offer and you know what the offices have to offer in turn. Now you have to apply.

## The Application

Your application package should begin with the cover letter, follow with your résumé (including names of your references) and finally include a mini-portfolio. Each of these parts of your application will need to be attractive, focused, as well as easy to read and handle. Architectural offices, especially the well-known ones, sometimes process hundreds of applications a month, so your work and credentials need not only to stand out, but also avoid frustrating the person who is looking at your package. Each part of the application package needs to be simple for another reason. Unless you have existing strengths in a niche area, or there is a shortage of architectural employees (this can happen in an economic boom but is rarer that you might think), or have researched the offices to whom you are applying and you know there is a good match between you, it is entirely possible that you will be sending out 100 job applications or more. Making a complex portfolio and résumé will make it very expensive for you to copy and mail each package.

### *Application Letter*

Your cover letter should be short and clear, stating who you are, for which position you are applying, why you are applying, and why you hope you will be able to make a positive contribution to the office. It should have clear contact details – your address, phone number, and e-mail address if you have one. It should also be simple and pleasing to the eye. Form letters will tell the office that you are not really interested in working for them. Whether or not you send out a large number of applications "on spec", research about a particular office, like research about a school, is essential, as it will help you at the very least adjust your application letter, and highlight certain aspects of your résumé. Call each office before you apply, ask to speak to the person who selects candidates for interview and enquire about the kind of application materials she/he will want to see, as well as when and how they are reviewed. This kind of research will show that you are serious about your application, and will give you a much better idea how to adjust your application to suit the office. If you get no return call, give up – call again until you get clear information, whether positive or negative. Persistence may lead you to be offered an interview, even if there is no work at the time. It is not that unusual for an interview to lead to a job offer later on – offices can keep details of outstanding candidates for some time and call back when work comes in (make sure that if you move, you pass on your new contact details – particularly easy to forget if you are finishing either your undergraduate or graduate degree).

Or, you may call on just the day that the office has received a significant commission and needs help.

## Résumé

Your résumé should also be clear and attractive. It should not be longer than two pages and be printed on thicker, better quality paper that the cover letter so that it stands out by its weight and quality. It can include colour if that helps the clarity of the communication process or makes the kind of visual impression you want to make. The reason it has to be short is that it is a résumé, not a CV. It is a summary whereas a CV is exactly what it says, in Latin, the run of your life or your life's achievements. A bad résumé can lose you a job – if an office sees you cannot summarize your strengths easily, it will be concerned about your other communication skills and your ability to focus. Your résumé should show how the expertise and experience you have is relevant to the position for which you are interviewing. That may mean having different versions of the résumé, each emphasizing specific strengths in relation to the job you want.

Your résumé must be concise. It should be accurate and truthful, and free of grammar or spelling mistakes. Do not fudge anything, show your strengths and have someone with good English proofread it if you are unsure of your language skills. It can consist of a narrative or bullet format, or a combination of both. If it has narrative, this should be short and to the point. In the USA, it is not appropriate to include information about (or indeed be asked at interview about) your marital status, your age or health as this may be seen as discriminatory, so do not put such information on your résumé. Once you are offered the position, however, your employer may need such information to negotiate health insurance, etc. In the UK, however, job application forms often ask for such information so including it in your résumé is appropriate. As with the portfolio it is important to check for national differences in résumé writing through friends, professors, and advisors.

There are certain things that must be included on your résumé. At a minimum they should consist of:

- Your name, address, telephone number, e-mail address, and web page uniform resource locator (URL) if you have one.
- Your educational qualifications, dates of study, including the date you obtained your qualifications, and where you obtained them. If you won prizes include them in the appropriate time period.
- Your employment experience to date, including the names of your employers, the dates of employment, and a brief summary of the work

you did. For example: Project Architect – responsible for construction documents, construction administration, details, coordination of structural, and MEP (mechanical/electrical/plumbing) consultants, etc.

· Any other knowledge or experience you have that will help you get the job (e.g. being fluent in a foreign language if you are applying to an office with much of its work overseas, or community service if you are applying for a job in an office doing community architecture).

In many other employment areas references are not required on the résumé. In architecture, however, it may be as important whom you know (that will be able to vouch for your skills and personal characteristics) as what you know, so check with your interviewer how many references she/he requires (three is usual). If you do not list any of your former employers or professors as references, the person reading your résumé may assume that you have something to hide. Your last employer is usually the one you should put first on the list of references, as she/he will have most recent knowledge of you. It is *very* important to check with all of your references that they agree to do this for you before you list them, as it is possible that some will turn you down. If that is the case, do not be disheartened, and go on to ask the next person.

Finally, it is really helpful to re-read your résumé the day before the interview, so that you are ready for questions at the interview.

### Application Portfolio

The initial portfolio you attach with your application, the application portfolio, is the principal means of attracting the attention of the office and getting selected for interview. As with the academic portfolio, you should focus on what kind of a message this portfolio is trying to convey. What are the strengths of your work as a student and as a professional? How can you show your usefulness to this office succinctly in a four to eight page format? What evidence or promise of practical competence does your work show? Can you show a translation of design ideas into built work? How can your résumé help to support the application portfolio's contents? Can you find a related graphic layout, and can you include key elements from the résumé in this portfolio to aid the linkage? Can you do something very simple to tailor each portfolio at least in part to the focus of the particular office? How can you use colour, layout, text, drawings, and photos to capture the imagination of the person who may only have 10 or 20 seconds before they accept or reject your application? As with any architectural competition, the impression you make in the first 10 seconds is the most important.

## The Interview Portfolio

For details of how to prepare a portfolio for interview please read *The Portfolio: An Architecture Student's Handbook*, in the same series as this book.

### The Interview

Your skills, experience, and future potential will be the three main areas that any office will need to evaluate during the interview process. The interview portfolio should be able to address many of the skill-related questions. You should be able to refer to your résumé to elaborate verbally on the employment experience you have so far to the person who is interviewing you. If that person is not asking you questions that allow you to describe your strengths, try to lead the conversation in that direction. The evaluation of your potential is a much subtler issue. Surveys of architectural employers have shown that your ability to communicate, adapt, and fit in to the culture of an office are the most important evaluation categories in an interview. Your appeal to an office will therefore only partly consist of your portfolio and résumé. More important will be the character you demonstrate through your appearance and behaviour. An office knows that you will need to learn how that office works – and that to do this you will need to be a team player, to speak with clarity and confidence but also have a humility about your ideas, to show a willingness to listen, change and to learn, to care about your own competence, to have respect for others, to have a sense of humour, to be ethical, to show commitment to a project and work hard to turn it into reality – in short, that you can act as a professional. You can help to demonstrate that you can do all this in the way that you talk about your work at the interview, so you should make sure that you have some visual and verbal elements in the portfolio to remind you to do so. If you are able to show the office that you have done extensive research on the office's work, that the work in your portfolio fits some or many of its needs and interests, that you are punctual, reliable, and polite, that your appearance fits the office's dress and behaviour code (if you can find out what this is), and that you are willing to learn, it will all add to your attractiveness.

You will also need to be clear, though always very polite, about your hopes for and expectations of the position. You will always need to prepare carefully for an interview, but will need to take particular care with your internship interview, as you will need the right kind of experience to count towards your licensure or registration. That means you will need to be ready with the right kind of questions for the person who is interviewing you. At the interview you should therefore share the expectations that the architectural profession in your country places on the internship experience or the year out. Particularly if you are applying to an office abroad the person interviewing you may be unfamiliar with these expectations, so clarity will save a lot of headaches later on. It may be helpful for you to bring a list of the responsibilities you will be expected to experience during the course of a year or so, and ask your interviewer whether you would be likely to do that in the position. If the answer is evasive, you might think twice about continuing your interest in the position. You should always ask a lot of questions about the work of the office, preferably having already done some research, so that you can show you are prepared. At the interview you might ask about the office's projects, where the projects are, which of them you might join as a team member, what might be your responsibilities, who will be your supervisor, and so on.

At the end of the interview you should also ask some questions about employment conditions. If successful, would you be an employee, or is this a freelance position? What would be the benefits? What are the hours of work? What is the hourly rate, or weekly, monthly, or yearly salary? With respect to the salary, memorize the level of pay you are ideally seeking, as an hourly rate, and as weekly, monthly, or yearly salary. These will vary from employer to employer, and certainly from country to country. Ask who will pay your health, retirement, health or disability insurance? If it is a split commitment, who will pay how much? Be ready for some quick mental arithmetic. You will need to have done your homework to find out what is an appropriate level of pay, responsibility, and time commitment. Here you will most likely have to consult friends, and enlist the help of your mentor or professors for further contacts who may be able to tell you more so you are ready with the range of choices, the current standard practice if it exists, and the bottom line for you. Your local or regional professional organization may also give you some advice. That way you will know right away at the interview whether the job will provide the kind of financial support you need to survive.

Finally you should ask, if you were offered the position, when you would be expected to start. Some offices like to interview simply to maintain a pool of applicants, and may not actually have a position to offer you. If you do not get a clear answer about a start date, or a response that the office is waiting for confirmation from a client about a project, you should look for another position.

If there are no clear answers to some or all of these questions at the interview, you might consider writing a brief note to the office after a day of so to let them know that you are no longer available for employment. Lack of clarity indicates that later on an office may also not honour commitments to your Internship/Internship Development Program (IDP) needs. If you have a choice, take the position where your responsibilities and rewards are clear. You will gain not only good professional experience from a firm of that kind, but you should also learn integrity and sound business practice.

## The Job Offer and the Employment Agreement

You have had a number of interviews, you think they went well, and you are interested in more than one position. You therefore face the likelihood of discussing and agreeing an employment agreement, or the terms under which you will be hired and expected to work. You may even be at an interview where you are offered a job on the spot. Do not wait for an office to make an offer that you do not understand and need more advice to accept or reject. Saying "I need to think about this" or "can I call you back on this" makes you seem unprepared and by the time you decide the job may have been offered to someone else. Accepting an offer without understanding its terms makes you seem naïve and, more importantly, may hurt you later on. Make sure you know as much as you can about the kinds of components that an employer is likely to offer you, and be prepared to do more asking and some negotiating. Employers are not always prepared themselves – many may simply say "congratulations, you have the job!". You should express your delight at the offer, sound very excited, but should also definitely ask questions before you accept, and most importantly be ready to do so right away – not later.

First, if you were reasonably clear about explaining your year out/IDP needs during the interview, you should ask the office to confirm that it will be able to give you the range of experience you need. Most likely you will be attached to one or two projects, so ask more questions about how the office sees your role in these, which one will involve site visits, construction drawing experience, participation in clients' meetings, budgeting work, coordinating with consultants, and so on. Just in case you find asking all of these questions daunting, ask your mentor for a practice session.

Second, reconfirm with the office whether you will be an employee, or work freelance, whether this is a full-time or a part-time position, or whether you may be subcontracted to another office in the future. This last question is one few students ask, but it is becoming a more common practice, as offices share resources during difficult economic times. You may only get a verbal offer, and sometimes you may need to accept it. A verbal offer is still a contract, but is difficult to enforce, as memory is not always reliable.

Third, confirm working hours, especially expectations during major project deadlines, and whether the office offers overtime pay. Many offices expect employees to work late or over the weekend, if there is a pressing deadline and may not be very flexible in this area. This can discourage committed parents. If you have a family, you will need to know how to respond. If you are the main parenting person in a family, it may make the difference between taking or turning down a position.

Fourth, reconfirm the benefits offered to you, such as pension and health care when appropriate. Depending on your circumstances, these may not be that important. Make sure, if you have a family, that your family understands whatever compromises you are willing to make in this area in order to take the position as they may become directly affected by your decision.

Fifth, reconfirm the starting date of the position and ask whether there are any unusual conditions that the employer may not have discussed at the interview. You do not want any major surprises later on.

Finally, always talk in a positive, constructive, and respectful tone of voice, and listen to the answers. Every employer will understand your need for clarity. Take notes if it seems appropriate, and write down the detail of a telephone offer during the conversation, or if this is not possible, as soon as you can after you finish talking. If you sense the employer's offence at any of your questions, and you are sure of your civility and respect in asking them, ask politely if the particular issue is a problem, and allow the employer to explain. If you do not like the explanation, consider politely declining the offer even at that stage. Again, you may not have much of a choice, but as you may be committing a year or more of your life to the position, as well as the beginning of your professional career, if you are uneasy then you should follow your instincts.

### Pay and Conditions

In the UK, ARCHAOS is a useful resource for student architects. As well as offering networking opportunities, it is a powerful and influential body that works with the RIBA to ensure fair working conditions for student architects. Their paper on student architect employment, accepted by the RIBA Council in 2001, identifies recommended minimum conditions of employment and indicative rates of pay in the UK for a post-Part 1 Student Architect. It is recognized by the profession as an important guide for employers and students alike. At the time of going to print with this volume RIBA and ARCHAOS recommended an hourly rate for post-Part 1 Architectural Assistants of £5.60 per hour. This was adjusted for the extra expense experienced by students working in London to £6.70 per hour.

The RIBA states that an employer within the architectural profession has a legal responsibility to provide conditions of employment that conform to National Minimum Wage legislation and the European Union (EU) working directive. This includes providing you with a contract of employment, limiting your working week to a maximum of 48 hours[1] and paying at least the National Minimum Wage, which is (at the time of going to print with this volume) £4.10 per hour. If an architect employer does not adhere to these guidelines she/he may be disciplined by Architects' Registration Board (ARB)/RIBA for breach of the RIBA Code of Conduct or the ARB Code of Professional Conduct, which is in itself a breach of the Architects' Registration Act. The new RIBA template for professional experience employment contracts at Stages 1 and 2, published on the Professional Experience and Development Record (PEDR), provides clear guidance to both employers, and student and graduate employees on what they should expect to sign up to.

In the USA, compensation for intern architects varies from state to state, depending on the cost of living, status of economy and the number of hours you will be working. The AIA web site includes a salary chart for intern architects based on the AIA compensation reports (see below).

Resource

• AIA Salary charts: www.aia.org/idp/idpresources.asp

If at the end of all this you have reached agreement and, preferably, have signed a contract, then you are ready to start your job – congratulations!

---

[1]If asked to exceed this, you must be asked by your employer to sign a voluntary waiver, which you are legally entitled to refuse.

# 12   Office Cultures

In this chapter you will learn about the first steps in accommodating yourself to an office environment, how to get organized, and how to communicate effectively. We will also introduce some broader professional codes, norms, and expectations in an architectural office, emphasizing the importance of ethics in a professional setting.

## Getting Organized

An office is a collective enterprise, based on collaboration and team work. It is very important to be organized and in control of what you are doing on a day-to-day basis. You will also discover that honest and regular communication with your mentor/supervisor will greatly ease your transition to an office culture.

The practice of an architect requires clarity, precision, and careful record taking, whether it be a telephone message (who rang, when, what time, for whom, what was the extent of the information given, what did they expect, and when?), details of conversations at a meeting, or the accuracy of a survey drawing. It is therefore highly recommended that you keep a diary. This will prove useful for completing your Professional Experience and Development Record (PEDR)/Internship Development Program (IDP) and will be a record of what you have done on a daily basis. It can be used to help clarify instructions given to you by a member of the practice as well as proving an invaluable record of how the office operates, how decisions are made and problems dealt with. You should, however, be careful not to spend your days writing your diary or IDP council records, it is for you to complete in your own time. Many year out students and interns use their lunch break for that or choose to complete it at the end of the day.

It is good practice to prepare for all meetings well in advance, be they with the design team within the office, with the broader construction/consultant teams or with your Professional Advisor or Employment Mentor (Supervisor or Mentor in the USA). Make notes about anything that you would like to raise, the content of your points and any relevant information. Be clear about what you want to say, be polite and appropriately assertive and never lose your temper. In the case of design or consultant meetings, or a meeting with your Professional Advisor, you may want to discuss your points with your Employment Mentor first. It may also be appropriate for you to discuss a meeting with your Employment Mentor in advance with your Professional Advisor. If in doubt, ask, but ensure that you know when they are available for you to contact them. Professional Advisors often have a time slot when you can speak to them on the telephone or you may have to make an appointment via their secretary. It may be a good idea to arrange a regular meeting time with your Employment Mentor and also make an arrangement for telephone calls should you need immediate advice.

Some offices will supply you with a copy of their employee manual, personal policy manual or office procedures guidelines when you are hired. You should keep to these rules whenever you can. If you have additional questions, ask your supervisors or, if you are in a large firm, talk to the Human Resources Department. These rules could relate to getting drawings printed, using filing systems, obtaining employment verification letters or learning how the office library operates. By being informed you will be able to learn more and create a good impression.

## Taking Responsibility for Learning

As a student or an intern you will be expected to take responsibility for your learning, so that by the end of your training, you will be skilled and ready to sit and pass the professional examination and understand the responsibilities of an independently practising registered architect. You will also be expected to embark on your Continuing Professional Development (CPD) in the UK, or Mandatory Continuing Education (MCE) in the USA.[1] Working in a practice is a particularly useful opportunity to

---

[1] CPD in the UK, or MCE in the USA, ensure that practising registered architects maintain their professionalism and competence throughout their careers. The necessity for "lifelong learning" is deemed essential for a responsible career as an architect and is recognized as a mechanism for consumer protection.

identify the types of activities in which architects later engage to fulfil their CPD requirement. This is important if you are a UK student as, if you visit the Royal Institute of British Architects (RIBA) web site, you will see that CPD is self-directed and it is up to you to tailor to suit your own career ambitions and workload requirements. All architects are, of course, expected to continue with their CPD/MCE studies following registration.

Taking responsibility for your own learning within an office environment means that you should watch for opportunities to learn new areas of architectural expertise. You should consult your office supervisor/ mentor and, having gained his/her support, do not be shy to politely ask to do this work if your office is not giving you the opportunity. This also means that you will need to take your work seriously and, when involved in new activities, often take extra time outside of office time to research the knowledge you might need. And you will of course be expected to be reliable and responsible throughout your employment. One of the most frequent criticisms that employers have of students is lack of punctuality. Even if your office is a friendly and relaxed one, always make sure you act as professionally as possible and come to meetings a few minutes early. Do not forget that you may need a good reference for your next job, and also may wish to return to that firm to work at some later point of time. Even if neither happens, if you develop a good relationship with your first office, you may find you have a willing mentor in its members for many, many years.

## Getting Really Good Experience

Identifying the kind of experience and skills you have gained and what may still be lacking is fundamental to your education and offers you the potential to act where experience is not as broad or "hands on" as it should be. Acting on this can be as simple as showing your Supervisor/ Employment Mentor your IDP/PEDR whilst identifying areas you have not yet experienced and need to do so. To do this effectively and professionally, it is advisable to prepare yourself well for this kind of meeting: think about the different jobs being undertaken in the office, what stages they are at and suggest how you might get involved. Although being a participant in an activity is always preferable, being an observer is also useful to your education. Listening, as well as doing, is an important skill to learn.

You may wish to talk to your Supervisor/Employment Mentor on an informal basis first, in order to gain his/her support. If possible, ask them to accompany you to any meetings in which your responsibilities are discussed and agreed. Finally, when discussing your experience and responsibilities, remember to always be constructive – try to share with the office how you will be much more useful to them with the additional skills and experience they can give you. Negotiating is one of the most important skills you can learn, and having a range of solutions you can politely offer to a problem you perceive to exist may help your office help you. However, as a beginning employee, also be prepared for some disappointments; if these occur repeatedly, and the economic climate allows it, move on to another position. Some offices are famous for treating students as cheap computer "fodder", others are fantastic at exposing students to high-level experience.

Many students find it difficult to negotiate within the office context. Make sure that if you can, you speak to your mentor every day. Although this is not always practicable, it is a very good habit to get into; by keeping each other informed, issues or concerns are far less likely to build up and become problems. Always be polite, but explain if you are unhappy or confused. Be constructive about any criticisms you may have about your role within the office. Do not just complain – suggest ways your Supervisor/Employment Mentor or the office may be able to deal with your concerns.

Always take any criticism from your Employment Mentor in the spirit it is given. Most architects want to help students to succeed and constructive (and occasionally negative) criticism may sometimes necessary. You may not always be aware that you are doing something inappropriate. The impact of body language in particular can sometimes be significant, especially as it tends to be subconscious and therefore you may not be aware of it or its effects.

If you do find that your work or conduct is being criticized, ask for help and guidance in putting it right. No one is perfect and we all make mistakes, but how you respond to criticism is important in maintaining good office relations, and sometimes to keeping your job as well.

Demonstrate that you want to learn and work hard. Make an effort to do extra work/research outside of office hours to enable you to be informed and reasonably knowledgeable about what you are doing. However, do not feel that because your supervisor or mentor works late every day means that you must do the same. Of course, if there is a deadline and everyone is working flat out to get a drawing package or preparations for a presentation finished, it would be seen as positive that you too are prepared to contribute any help that you can. But as an architectural assistant you will not normally be expected be work late and you may wish to discuss and change the situation if you are asked to do so. This is particularly important if you have a family and need to balance your personal and professional time. Always approach your mentor in the first instance about such issues to enlist their help. Some American firms also have official mentor/ protégé programmes, which help you understand and cope with the corporate environment. These programmes are offered in addition to your IDP mentorship, exposing you to more opinions and points of view about the profession. This arrangement can provide another, hopefully good, listener for any issues that you might have in your professional life.

## Codes, Norms, and Expectations

Even though each office has its own specific expectations of its employees, most still follow common guidelines in organizing and running their day-to-day operations. It is a shared responsibility between you and your supervisor to understand what the codes, norms and expectations are. After you start working, you may want to talk to your colleagues and get further tips and unofficial advice as to what the reality of your office is, what your supervisors prefer and what is the typical response to those preferences by most of your peers. Many firms, especially larger firms, provide orientation sessions for their new hires, giving you an opportunity to familiarize yourself with the culture of a particular firm, its norms and expectations. Depending on the size of the firm and the complexity of its business operations, these orientation sessions might take up to several full days. In large firms such orientations are usually conducted by the Human Resources Department, a part of the firm that oversees all hiring and termination procedures, as well as providing everyday support for employees (vacation and sick leave forms, benefits, verification of employment letters, etc.). The Human Resources Department is usually the first place to which questions you are referred in case you have a query regarding the administration aspect of your business. You should feel free to ask not only during orientation sessions, but even later as you become a more experienced member of your firm's community. Some firms might also send you more information regarding their policies together with their job offer letter, thus preparing you for your first day at work. Other firms might have a *Personal Policy Manual*, which may contain all information regarding your employer's expectations. In small offices you will mainly be expected to pick things up as you go along.

### Attendance and Punctuality

Attendance policies are something you should already discuss during your interview, even before you start working in a particular office. You need to verify the official business hours of the firm, during which you are required to be at your desk working. A typical workday is 8 hours, Monday through Friday, with the exception of observed holidays. You might also find many regional variations as to how these 8 hours are being used during the day. In the UK, most firms are officially open from 9:00 a.m. to 6:00 p.m., with a 1 hour unpaid lunch break. In the USA, most firms are open from 8:00 a.m. to 5:00 p.m., also with a 1 hour lunch break. The lunch break hour is usually unpaid, but you will notice that some firms are changing their policies and pay for their employees for a half-an-hour lunch break, while the other 30 minutes is seen as your own unpaid time. Some public institutions and local government offices have fully paid lunch breaks, which counts towards your 8 hours spent at work. In some other parts of the world, the tradition of "siesta", or taking a nap after a lunch is still observed, which leads to a much longer lunch break of 2 or sometimes even 3 hours. Although a longer lunch break might seem like a good idea, as a result you will be spending more time at work – 10 or 11 hours together with your break. Most state laws in the USA, require employers to provide a lunch break to those employees scheduled to work a minimum of 7.5 consecutive hours in a day.

In some instances, a firm might offer flexible hours, asking employees to work during core hours (e.g. from 9:00 a.m. to 4:00 p.m.) and then working the rest of the necessary hours at the employees discretion either before or after core hours (or a combination of thereof). Other offices might have special summer hours, during which employees work 9 hours a day Monday through Thursday, and then only 4 hours Friday morning, thus allowing for a slightly longer weekend. Most firms however, will not allow you to "bank" hours; that is, work 10 hours and 4 days a week, and then not work on Friday, or work during the weekend or at owl hours and then not show up for work during core business hours. Finally, daily starting times vary from firm to firm, so make sure you confirm with your supervisor when are you expected to show up in the morning, and make sure you are there on time (or preferably a little bit early).

In addition to a lunch break, some firms may or may not provide additional employee breaks or rest periods, such as refreshment and snack breaks, coffee breaks, etc. Most firms however, will consider these as a personal time taken by employees during the day, which is expected to be made up in that same day, or within that pay period. This also applies to extended lunch hours (the so-called "long lunch"), health care appointments, personal business (banking, post office), etc.

In negotiating your contract or oral terms of employment, you will be informed of the number or sick or vacation days that you may be able to use per year. You are expected to report in advance any use of vacation days, and in case of sick days, to inform your supervisor within a couple of hours of the usual start time (but, the sooner, the better) via voice mail or e-mail.

The recording of your work days may vary significantly between firms. Some companies have weekly or bi-weekly timesheets that you are required to fill out each week or pay period, itemizing the number of hours spent on each project every day. These timesheets can be prepared as paper forms, or can also be used as digital forms that can be submitted online. Some firms even have an automated monitoring system on your computer, a network system that automatically records your activity at your workstation, calculating the number of hours spent on each file or a project. Timesheets are also used to record any use of sick or vacation days. More traditional offices might still use punch cards, thus recording the time you came in and left your desk. Smaller firms will often operate on the honour system with respect to sick or vacation days, but also will most likely require you to fill in timesheets for billing purposes. In all cases, firms operate on the basis of profit and efficiency, making sure not only that you spent your required time at work, but also that you are using the time that you are paid for in the most efficient way.

## Dress Codes

Various firms can have different dress code policies, depending on the size of the firm, its culture, tradition, and types of work. In establishing a certain dress policy, the company wants to make sure that each employee is successfully representing the company in its entirety. The bottom line is that appearance is important. Being over- or under-dressed can be rather uncomfortable for you as well as the clients of the office.

### Corporate or Business Formal Dress Code

Traditionally, many architectural offices used to have a very formal dress code. Today, this code is still present in some firms, although as an intern or a year-out student you may still be allowed to dress more casually than long-term employees. You must check with your supervisor as to how are you expected to dress for work each day. Corporate or business formal dress code for men includes wearing a suit (matching jacket and trousers) with a button-down shirt and a tie. For women, this also means wearing a suit, but it is acceptable to wear either trousers or a skirt; a button-down shirt is also the "most formal," but typically not required. Generally speaking, if the dress code is corporate, it is best to err on the "more formal" side of your clothing collection.

### Corporate Casual or Business Casual Dress Code

In order to create a more relaxed and stimulating work environment, many companies are switching their dress policies to corporate casual, which means that employees are not required to wear business suits, ties and dresses. This means that employees can enjoy a more comfortable work atmosphere, while still maintaining a professional and respectable image of a firm. It is however important to emphasize that this does not mean that you will never have to wear a business suit. As with everything else, common sense and careful examination of your daily schedule will lead you to decide when business attire is appropriate or necessary. For example, client meetings or important presentations are typical instances when traditional business clothing is appropriate. Bear in mind that not all casual clothing is appropriate for the firm. "Corporate casual" is very different from "weekend casual", meaning that torn blue jeans and worn tennis shoes are most probably more appropriate for your weekend outings than for the workplace. If you are not sure if an item of clothing is acceptable, either choose something else or simply ask your supervisor ahead of time. Some of the generally accepted types of corporate casual clothing for men include: khakis (the style, not the colour) and other smart casual trousers, button-down shirts, cleanly pressed sport shirts, blazers, sport coats, sweaters, vests, dress shirts and ties, loafers, or similar shoes. Some of the generally accepted types of corporate casual clothing for women include: casual dresses, skirts and blouses, smart trousers, blazers, jackets, sweaters, vests, skirts, loafers, pumps and dress sandals. The following items are not considered appropriate for most workplaces for both men and women: work-out clothes (including lycra, running tights, shorts, tank tops, sweat pants, and shirts), jeans, worn, torn, faded or stained clothing, halter tops, athletic shirts or T-shirts, thong or beach sandals, gym or sport shoes.

### Casual Friday

In addition to having an official dress policy, a company with a corporate casual dress code might also implement a concept of a so-called "Casual

Friday", allowing its employees to wear even more casual clothing, including jeans and T-shirts. This however still means that all of your clothing must be clean and nicely pressed. Worn, torn, faded or stained clothes are not appropriate even for a Casual Friday.

*Business Appropriate*

Business appropriate is another trend in professional dressing. It means that you should dress appropriately for the day that is ahead of you. If you will be going out on the construction site, corporate casual or even casual might be appropriate; if you have a high-level meeting or presentation to a client, a suit is more appropriate. Remember that "Business Appropriate" involves shoes too. Wearing casual sandals is not appropriate for many firms.

### Phone and Computer Manners

A lot of architectural offices have an open floor plan, without physical barriers or separation between workstations. As a consequence, it is very important to adjust your voice to the environment while you are on the phone; loud phone conversations or inappropriate language do not leave good impression on your "neighbours". If you have your own office phone number, you will also need to record a greeting. This needs to be done professionally; you need to clearly say your name and the name of the company. Some firms might even give you a recommended greeting that you should record. Also, if you plan to be away from the office for a longer period of time, more than a week or so, it is usually a good idea to change your greeting so it says that you are out of the office until certain date. Some offices will also recommend switching off your personal cell phone and only using your business phone (or a business cell phone in case you are given one). Other offices may ask you to use your cell phone only during permitted breaks to make personal calls. Remember that you should only use your company's phone for business purposes and only for urgent and/or brief personal matters, if your company has no cell phone permitted in the office.

Many large firms will have an Information Technology (IT) Department, which will take care of your computer needs, maintain your workstation, and come to help you with problems if needed. Some firms will even have AutoCAD hot lines, which you can call if you need help with using AutoCAD. Remember that, as with your office telephone, your office computer is your company's property and you should fully adhere with its policies. As with the dress code, use common sense, observe your environment, see what other people are doing and you should be fine. Remember that your computer workstation should be used for business purposes only. Most firms will reserve the right to monitor all of its computer activities, including files, flow of information on the Internet, downloading or taking out the software, etc. Some firms might even have automated billing software, which automatically counts the amount of time spent on a certain CAD file, so they can bill the client directly. As a consequence, your productivity is highly visible. Remember that casual surfing on the Internet, including shopping, is not acceptable. If you must do it, gain the office's permission beforehand, and do it either during lunch hour or after hours. However, web surfing that involves obscene, pornographic, harassing, unlawful material is not acceptable at any time. Finally remember that copyrighted materials such as MP3 or MPEG files should not be stored or reproduced on any of the computers in your firm. Some firms will also let you legally install some of the firm's software products on your home computer, if their software license allows them to do so. This can help you in case you need to do some additional work at home and want to avoid staying very late at work.

## Collegiality and Professional Conduct

Every architectural firm is founded on the premise that architectural practice is a team effort. Therefore, a "team attitude" is strongly encouraged in order to provide the best service and the best and most comfortable environment. This mean that as an intern or a year-out student you should feel a part of the team, respect the rights and opinions of others and share knowledge openly with your colleagues. You must also respect the confidentiality of all professional and personal information that is accessible to you within the firm. Such information includes documents, correspondence with clients, contractors, etc.

### Socializing With Your Colleagues and Balancing Your Personal Life

Work in a firm brings with it a new quality to your social life. You will often be asked by your colleagues to join then for a "happy hour" or a similar social event after the work. Do not feel obliged to create new "best friends", but do socialize with your colleagues if you can. Social events are, like the projects themselves, part of a team attitude. Some, particularly larger firms, might have very structured social life, or a particular firm culture. This can involve dinner parties, golf outings, annual parties for employees and their partners, etc. It is a good idea to participate as much as you can, but do not feel stretched or obliged to attend everything. Especially if you have a family or are about to start one, learning how to balance personal and professional life is very important. Many employers are increasingly recognising that they can improve the performance and well-being of their employees, including young interns and year-out students, by helping them achieve a balance between their job and personal life. If a lack of balance becomes an issue, make sure to discuss it with your supervisor. Flexible work arrangements (including flexible work hours and days), part-time work, job sharing, work from home, and paid parental leave are some examples of family friendly practices that can help protect your personal life or family obligations. Having said this, many architectural offices still have cultures of long hours, which can be hard if you are committed to family life. This kind of culture is one of the reasons why there are still so few women in the architectural profession. This situation is changing slowly, and if this is important to you, sharing your concerns about this with your supervisor/mentor is critical.

## Equal Employment Opportunity Legislation

As you are entering the workforce you should familiarize yourself with some basic terminology and legislation that deals with human and civil rights principles. Employment Opportunity Legislation protects principles of non-discrimination and equal employment opportunity for all people, regardless of their sex, race, age, colour, religion, national origin, ethnicity, sexual orientation, pregnancy, disability, veteran status, and other protected characteristics as required by relevant laws. Like other entities, architectural companies are obliged to adhere to these laws and advance their principles through all aspects of the employment relationship, including recruitment, hiring, compensation, fringe benefits, training, advancement and discharge. In the USA, the Equal Employment Opportunity Commission (EEOC) enforces federal laws that prohibit job discrimination, providing oversight, and coordination of all federal equal employment opportunity regulations, practices, and policies. In the UK, the Equal Opportunities Commission has similar oversight of the situation.

Sexual harassment is an area of particular concern for many companies. Many large companies will organize seminars for new employees that deal with the prevention of sexual harassment. Sexual harassment includes various forms of verbal or physical behaviour of a sexual nature when:

1. submitting or refusing to submit to such conduct is used as a basis for any employment-related decision, and/or;
2. such conduct has the purpose or an effect of creating an intimidating and hostile professional environment.

It is important to respect *others*, bearing in mind that some forms of behaviour that might be appropriate for social settings, are not acceptable in an office. Sexual harassment can affect both men and women, and people of different or same sex. It includes unwelcome social advances, verbal harassment, vulgar jokes, physical harassment, including touching or threatening to touch, and the distribution of written or graphic sexual material. Make sure to familiarize yourself with your firm's harassment policies, and if you feel that you have been a victim make sure to bring that up with your supervisors. In some cases, what may seem common sense to you may not seem so to others. If you have moved to work in another country you may well find that you will need to adjust some of your common sense expectations, but in no case you should engage in activity you consider to be unethical, even if there is subtle or unsubtle pressure around you to do so.

Racial harassment is another area where subtle or unsubtle discrimination can occur. Racial harassment is seen to exist when considerations of race, ethnicity, and nationality are used to create a hostile working environment and are used as a basis for any employment-related decision. Age, and sexual orientation are also included in many countries as equal opportunity issues that should not impact the work environment and employment-related policies.

Resources

- UK Equal Opportunities Commission: www.eoc.org.uk
- USA Equal Employment Opportunity Commission: www.eeoc.gov
- Australian Human Rights and Equal Opportunities Commission: www.hreoc.gov.au
- Equal Opportunities Commission, Hong Kong: www.eoc.org.hk
- Equal Employment Opportunities Trust, New Zealand: www.eeotrust.org.nz
- International Labour Organisation, United Nations: www.ilo.org

# 13   Afterwards

In this final chapter, we will discuss your life after the year out or internship year. We will also discuss the predicament of losing or changing a job, and introduce you to some of the professional educational opportunities ahead of you.

## Coping with the Termination of Employment

You had a great year out; your internship was exciting and rewarding. Eventually, your experience in an office terminated, either voluntarily or involuntarily. Knowing how best to handle termination of either kind is very important for your future career. If you decide to leave an office, make sure that you resign as gracefully as possible, leaving behind friends and future mentors. You never know when you may need a good reference for one of your jobs in the future, or may wish to return to that firm to work at some later point in time. Even if neither happens, if you develop a good relationship with your first office, you may find you have a willing mentor for many years to come. As with other office procedures make sure to check what the termination policies are. For a large office, the personnel policy manual will usually outline those procedures. In a small office finding out the norms is a little more awkward, as you will probably need to ask.

In some instances, the firm will require specific advance notice, 1 week, 2 weeks, etc. Most firms will require that you to resign in writing. Let your resignation letter be as amicable and optimistic as possible, thanking your supervisors and colleagues for all the help and support that they provided. You will want to talk to your supervisor first, and in a bigger firm, you will also be directed to an exit interview with your supervisor and a human resources specialist who will help you understand the termination policies related to compensation and continuation of your benefits, if applicable. In this interview you can also discuss details of your reasons for leaving and ask questions about housekeeping matters, such as returning any company property (manuals, cell phones, etc.), the conversion/rollover of your health insurance[1], accrued vacation time and sick days, etc. It is also wise to provide a forwarding address, in case you are moving to another town or country. Some firms will also arrange for your incoming e-mails to be forwarded to your new e-mail account for a certain period of time. Your supervisor will let you know if you need to finish any work that you are currently working on. Every separation is hard for both parties, but your employer will understand that as an intern you need to move on to new challenges and opportunities. It is of mutual benefit that the terminating employee takes into the community a feeling of goodwill toward the firm.

Unfortunately, not all termination of employments will come on your terms or be pleasant. Your firm can initiate an involuntary termination of employment, which includes laying you off for lack of work when the firm reduces its work force for economic or other reasons, and when there is no reasonable expectancy of being rehired within the foreseeable future. In some instances, an employee can be discharged for being incapable of performing the work, or due to a misconduct, misrepresentation or gross negligence. If you are a dedicated and hard-working intern or a year-out student, you should not fit into this category. However, you never know when the economy might slow down and bring your position into jeopardy. Even though you are a loyal team player in an office, it is good to keep your options open, even when you are happy at work. Always keep networking and examining other exciting opportunities for work.

Some firms may provide a severance pay to employees whose separation is initiated by the firm (unless, of course, you are fired for a cause, e.g. such as misconduct). Being laid off is hard, even for an experienced professional. Try to cope with this situation as gracefully as possible.

---

[1]In the USA, most of your benefits will cease with your last day of employment, while the extended medical and dental privileges are available to the terminated employee under Consolidated Omnibus Budget Reconciliation Act (also known as COBRA Act). You can learn more about the COBRA Act from the US Department of Labour web site at: http://www.dol.gov/dol/topic/health-plans/cobra.htm (accessed September 6, 2004).

In some bigger companies, you will be required to leave the office the same day and might even be denied access to your workstation. Do not take these actions personally; they are designed to prevent angry responses and are applicable to everyone. Make sure you leave your employer on good terms.

## Where Does Your Job Lead You To?

There are many answers to this question. Some people prefer to go back to school and pursue graduate studies. Your "back to school" option might involve moving abroad, experiencing learning in new contexts. You may consider work in other allied design disciplines, such as landscape architecture, planning, interior design, etc. In most cases, you will want to move to another office, now as a registered architect, and change types of project and the level of responsibility you have. A lot of young professionals and recent licensees are often tempted to start their own practice. This is an exciting option that you may want to consider, but being on your own means that you have to create stronger mentorship networks and have enough funds, and a clear business plan, to make it through uncertain beginnings. Your networks during your year out or internship year may lead to friendships with colleagues who might become your partners or important mentors in an independent practical endeavour.

The corporate ladder has titles such as an intern, architectural assistant, architect, associate, associate principal, principal, and chief executive officer. These usually reflect experience and level of responsibility. If you decide to move on to another firm, you should consider being promoted, either in terms of salary or in terms of rank, or both.

Your practical experience will also lead you into a complex network of the architectural profession, one that involves conventions, lectures, seminars, and memberships in professional associations. In addition to the Royal Institute of British Architects (RIBA) or the American Institute of Architects (AIA), many architects join other, more or less formal associations, centred on certain common interests or goals. These are important not only for learning, but also for networking; your colleagues in related professions can often become sources of work.

## Giving Back

As you read this book, you are most probably only thinking about the year out or internship, and it is very early for you to picture yourself as a registered professional. Yet even at this early stage in your career, you need to think of professional ethics in much broader terms, or to paraphrase the famous words of politicians, "think about what can you do for your profession, not only what your profession can do for you". Many registered architects volunteer to be mentors to recent graduates, and although this is a voluntary and time-consuming effort, it is very rewarding. By becoming someone's mentor, you are giving back to your professional community and ultimately you influence the future of the profession by helping to shape a new generation of architects.

We have talked about the role of critical theory in critical architectural practice. By giving back to professional and broader community you extend critical theory's ideals of empowerment of other people, and help support equal access to all professions. Many architects are involved with community organizations or work with school children to expose them to the profession of architecture and provide services that would otherwise not be available. Since you will be the representatives of a new generation of architects (or almost architects) you should consider giving back generously and introduce architecture to those who typically do not consider it as a part of their lives. After all, how else would they know about the rewarding world of *practical architectural experience*?

SECTION FOUR: APPENDICES

# Appendix A: Readings on Practice

Useful general readings about professional architectural practice and professionalism:

*AIA Code of Ethics and Professional Conduct*, AIA: Offfice of General Counsel, 1997, www.E-architect.com/institute/codeethics.asp

Barnett, J., Zoning, mapping and urban renewal as urban design techniques in *An Introduction to Urban Design* (New York: Harpers and Row); pp. 57–75

Blau, J., *Architects and Firms* (Cambridge, MA: MIT Press, 1984)

Boyer, E., *Building Community* (New York: Carnegie Foundation, 1996)

Boyle, B., Architectural practice in America in *The Architect*, Kostof, S. (ed.) (New York: Oxford University Press, 1977); pp. 309–344

Cuff, D., *Architecture: The Story of Practice* (Cambridge, MA: MIT Press, 1991)

Frampton, K., Towards an urban landscape in *Denatured Visions*, Adams, W. and Wrede, S. (eds) (New York: MoMA, 1993)

Groak, S., *The Idea of Building* (London: E&F.N.Spon, 1992)

Gutman, R., Two discourses of architectural educations in *Practices 3/4* (Cincinnati. University of Cincinnati Press, 1997); pp. 11–19

Gutman, R., Professions and their discontents: the psychodynamics of architectural practice in *Practices 5/6* (Cincinnati: University of Cincinnati Press, 1997); pp. 15–23

Gutman, R., *Architectural Practice: A Critical View* (Princeton: Princeton Architectural Press, 1988)

Kostof, S., *The Architect; Chapters in the History of the Profession* (New York: Oxford University Press, 1977)

Kotler, P., Social foundations of marketing: meeting human needs in *Principles of Marketing* (New Jersey: Prentice Hall, 1986); Chapter 1, pp. 3–24

Lewis, R.K., *Architect? A Candid Guide to the Profession* (Cambridge, MA: MIT Press, 1985)

Maddox, D. (ed.), *All About Old Buildings*, National Trust for Historic Preservation (Washington DC: Preservation Press, 1985)

Malnar, J., *The Interior Dimension* (New York: Van Nostrand Reinhold, 1992)

Rüedi, K., Curriculum vitae: the architect's cultural capital: educational practices and financial investments in *Occupying Architecture*, Hill, J. (ed.) (London: Routledge, 1998); pp. 23–37

Pile, J., *Interior Design* (New York: H.M. Abrams, 1995); Chapter 1

Saint, A., *The Image of the Architect* (New Haven: Yale University Press, 1983)

Sarfatti Larson, M., *Behind the Postmodern Facade* (London: University of California Press, 1993)

Sarfatti Larson, M., *The Rise of Professionalism: A Sociological Analysis* (Berkeley: University of California Press, 1977)

Saunders, W., *Reflections on Architectural Practices in the Nineties* (Princeton: Princeton Architectural Press, 1996)

Schmertz, M., Preface, *New Life for Old Buildings* (New York: McGrawHill, 1982)

Stevens, G., *The Favored Circle: The Social Foundation of Architectural Distinction* (Cambridge, MA: MIT Press, 1995)

Williamson, R.K., *American Architects and the Mechanics of Fame* (Austin: University of Texas Press, 1991)

# Appendix B: Resources for Information on International Architectural Practice

Each of the web sites below has links to other professional organizations that may lead you to interesting practices, allow you to research emerging areas, and in some instances find jobs. The following web sites were accessible in December 2003.

## International

| | |
|---|---|
| UIA | International Union of Architects |
| | http://www.uia-architects.org |
| CAA | Commonwealth Association of Architects |
| | http://www.comarchitect.org |
| IEASTE | International Association for the Exchange of Students for Technical Experience |
| | http://www.iaeste.org/ |

## North America

### Canada

| | |
|---|---|
| RAIC | Royal Architectural Institute of Canada |
| | http://www.raic.org |

## USA

NCARB   National Council of Architectural Registration Boards
        http://www.ncarb.org
AIA     American Institute of Architects
        http://www.aia.org
SARA    Society of American Registered Architects
        http://www.sara-national.org
The American Indian Council of Architects and Engineers
        http://www.aicae.org/

## Central and South America

### Argentina

FADEA   Federacion Argentina de Entidades de Arquitectos
        http://fadea.org.ar

### Barbados

BIA     Barbados Institute of Architects
        http://www.biabarbados.org

### Bolivia

CAB     Colegio de Arquitectos de Bolivia
        http://www.oarquitectosbolivia.org

### Brazil

IAB     Instituto de Arquitetos do Brasil
        http://www.aib.org.br

### Chile

CA      Colegio de Arquitectos de Chile
        http://www.coarq.com

### Dominican Republic

CODIA   Colegio Dominicano de Ingenieros, Arquitectos
        Agrimensores
        http://www.codia.org.do

**Honduras**

CAH        Colegios de Arquitectos de Honduras
http://www.e-cah.org

**Jamaica**

JIA        Jamaican Institute of Architects
http://www.jia.org.jm

**Mexico**

FCARM      Federacion de Colegios de Arquitectos Mexico
http://www.arquired.com.mx/fcarm/indice.htm

**Panama**

SPIA       Sociedad Panamena de Ingenieros y Arquitectos
http://www.multired.com/spia/spia1.htm

**Paraguay**

APAR      Asociacion Paraguaya de Arquitectos
http://www.apar.com.py

**Puerto Rico**

CAAPPR   Colegio de Arquitectos y Arquitectos Paysajistas
De Puerto Rico
http://www.caappr.com

**Suriname**

UAS       Union of Architects in Suriname
http://www.uas.sr.org

**Trinidad and Tobago**

TTIA       Trinidad and Tobago Institute of Architects
http://www.ttiarch.com

**Uruguay**

SAU       Sociedad de Arquitectos del Uruguay
http://www.sau.org.uy

# Europe

## *General*

ACE    Architects' Council of Europe
http://www.ace-cae.org

## *Andorra*

COAA    Collegi Oficial d'Arquitectes d'Andorra
http://www.coaa.ad

## *Austria*

OIAV    Oesterreichscher Ingenieur- und Architekten Verein
http://www.oaiv.at

## *Belgium*

OA    Orde van Architecten Belgie/Ordre des Architectes Belgiques
http://www.ordevanarchitecten.be

NAV    de Vlaamse Architectenorganisatie
http://www.nav.be

## *Bulgaria*

UAB    Union of Bulgarian Architects
http://www.bulgarianarchitects.org

## *Croatia*

HKAIG    Hrvatska Komora Arhitekata I Inzenjera U Graditeljstvu
http://www.hkaig.hr

## *Czech Republic*

CKA    Ćeska Komora Architektů
http://www.cka.cc

## *Denmark*

DAL-AA    Federation of Danish Architects
http://www.dal-aa.dk

**Finland**

SAFA        Finnish Association of Architects
            http://www.safa.fi

**France**

L'Ordre des Architectes
            http://www.architectes.org

**Germany**

BDA         Bund Deutsche Architekten
            http://www.bda.baunetz.de

**Greece**

TEE         Technical Chamber of Greece
            http://www.tee.gr

**Hungary**

MESZ        Magyar Epitomuveszek Szovetsege
            http://www.meszorg.hu

**Iceland**

AI          Association of Icelandic Architects
            http://www.ai.is

**Ireland**

RIAI        Royal Institute of Architects of Ireland
            http://www.riai.ie

**Italy**

CNAPPC      Consiglio Nazionale degli Architetti, Pianificatori,
            Paesaggisti e Conservatori
            http://www.cnappc.orchiworld.it

**Luxembourg**

OAI   L'Ordre des Architectes et des Ingenieurs-Conseils
http://www.oai.lu

**The Netherlands**

BNA   Royal Institute of Dutch Architects
http://www.bna.nl

Archined
http://www.archined.nl

**Northern Ireland**

RSUA   Royal Society of Ulster Architects
http://www.rsua.org.uk

**Norway**

NAL   National Association of Norwegian Architects
http://www.mnal.no

**Poland**

SARP   Stowarzyszenie Architektow Polskich
http://www.sarp.org.pl

**Portugal**

OA   Ordem dos Arquitectos
http://www.aap.pt
http://novo.oasrs.org

**Russia**

UAR   The Union of Architects of Russia
http://www.uar.ru

**Scotland**

RIAS   Royal Incorporation of Architects in Scotland
http://www.rias.org.uk

**Serbia**

SAS      Savez Arhitekata Srbije
http://www.dab.org.yu

**Slovakia**

SKA      Slovenska Komora Architektov
http://www.archinet.sk/KomArch/index.acp

**Slovenia**

DAL      Drustvo Arhitektov Ljubljana
http://www.drustvo-arhitektov-lj.si

**Spain**

CSCAE      Consejo Superior de los Colegios de Arquitectos De Espana
http://www.cscae.com
for links to regional colegios in Spain go to
http://www.arquinex.es

**Sweden**

SA      Sveriges Arkitekter/Swedish Association of Architects
http://www.arkitekt.se
Smaller Swedish practices (in Swedish only)
http://www.arkitekt.nu

**Switzerland**

BSA      Bund Schweitzer Architekten/Federacion des Achitectes
Suisses/Federazione Architetti Svizzeri
http://www.architekten-bsa.ch

**UK**

RIBA      Royal Institute of British Architects
http://www.riba.org
http://www.architecture.com
ARB      Architects Registration Board
http://www.arb.org.uk

### Wales

RSAW    Royal Society of Architects in Wales
        http://www.architecture-wales.com

## Africa

### Ghana

GIA     Ghana Institute of Architects
        http://www.arcghana.org.gh

### South Africa

SAIA    The South African Institute of Architects
        http://www.saia.org.za

### Tunisia

OAT     Order of Architects of Tunisia
        http://www.oat-tn.org

## Asia

### Japan

AIJ     Architectural Institute of Japan
        http://www.aij.or.jp

### China

ASC     Architectural Society of China
        http://www.chinaasc.org/english/asc.php

### India

IIA     The Indian Institute of Architects
        http://www.iia-india.org

### Lebanon

Order of Engineers and Architects of Beirut
        http://www.ordre-ing-bey.org.lb

**Taiwan**

AIROC   Architectural Institute of the Republic of China
        http://www.airoc.org.tw

**Korea**

AIK     Architectural Institute of Korea
        http://www.aik.or.kr

**Singapore**

SIA     Singapore Institute of Architects
        http://www.sia.org.sg

**Malaysia**

PAM     Pertubuham Akitek Malaysia
        http://www.pam-my.org

**Hong Kong**

HKIA    Hong Kong Institute of Architects
        http://www.hkia.net

**Thailand**

ASA     Association of Siamese Architects under Royal Patronage
        http://www.asa.or.th

**Bangladesh**

IAB     Institute of Architects Bangladesh
        http://www.citechco.net/iabnet/

**Sri Lanka**

SLIA    Sri Lanka Institute of Architects
        http://www.architecturesrilanka.com

**Pakistan**

IAP     Institute of Architects Pakistan
        http://www.iap.com.pk

**Philippines**

UAP   United Architects of the Philippines
      http://www.united-architects.org

## Oceania

*Australia*

RAIA   Royal Australian Institute of Architects
       http://www.raia.com.au
AACA   Architects Accreditation Council of Australia Inc.
       http://www.aaca.org.au

*Fiji*

FAA   Fiji Association of Architects
      http://www.fijiarchitects.com

**New Zealand**

NZIA   New Zealand Institute of Architects Incorporated
       http://www.nzia.co.nz

For lists of other professional Institutions related to architecture go to
http://www.uia-architectes.org/texte/summary/p2b1.html
http://www.arb.org.uk/links/professional-bodies.shtml
http://www.bulgarianarchitects.org/uia_members.htm

# Index

216    *Index*